American Masala

ALSO BY SUVIR SARAN

Indian Home Cooking (with Stephanie Lyness)

American Masala

125 NEW CLASSICS FROM MY HOME KITCHEN

 **SUVIR SARAN**

WITH RAQUEL PELZEL

CLARKSON POTTER/PUBLISHERS

NEW YORK

Published in the United States by Clarkson Potter/Publishers,
an imprint of the Crown Publishing Group,
a division of Random House, Inc., New York.

www.crownpublishing.com
www.clarksonpotter.com

Clarkson N. Potter is a trademark and Potter and colophon are registered
trademarks of Random House, Inc.

Library of Congress Cataloging-in-Publication Data
Saran, Suvir.
American Masala: 125 new classics from my home kitchen / Suvir Saran
with Raquel Pelzel.
1. Cookery, Indic.   I. Pelzel, Raquel.   II. Title.
TX724.5.I4S2976 2007
641.5954—dc22   2006037005

ISBN 978-0-307-34150-1

Printed in China

Design by Margaret Hinders

10   9   8   7   6   5   4   3   2   1

First Edition

To Bhagat Saran Bhatnagar, my paternal grandfather, who I knew only briefly but inspires us through memories of his good deeds. Chaman Lal Bhardwaj, my maternal grandfather, who wows everyone with his unparalleled global vision and genius. Guru Saran, my father, for his wit, character, and sensible spirituality. Seema and her loving husband, Ajit, for giving the world Karun, my nephew who keeps us all on our toes with his great lust for learning and awe-inspiring brilliance. Samir for being a wonderfully supportive brother.

Charlie for his constant attention to any- and everything I could wish for and more.

And to all the men who have made generations of fine home and restaurant cooking possible, either by their work in the kitchen or through their loving support of the women who selflessly nurture, nourish, and provide for our kids—our future.

Contents

introduction

Masala is the Hindi term for spice—not just the spice that one adds to food but also the spice of life, the excitement and vibrancy that come from stimulating conversation and a house full of friends and family. As a chef and cook, I find inspiration everywhere, from the countries I visit, the people I meet, and the food I taste along the way. I have found that the beauty of masala lies in its ability to transcend borders and oceans and find a home in just about any cuisine. I have lived in America for nearly as long as I lived in India, and American classics like lasagna, corn bread, and cobblers are now as much a part of my culinary heritage as are dal and dosas. Applying the knowledge of spices I learned in my native India to American dishes is what I like to call American masala. It's my reality and it's how I cook at home.

To me, American cuisine represents a culture of food that blends spices, techniques, and ingredients from different parts of the globe to become something fresh and exciting yet comforting and homey. It is a melting pot of fast paced and slow cooked, of convenience and tradition. It is about being free to play with new flavors and ideas. Having grown up in a country that is as old as time, yet still as young and fearless as a forward-moving nation can be, has given me a unique perspective on life. I create food that I love to eat, food that I find stimulating and satisfying, food that gets people talking.

It's often not traditional Indian food that I am cooking, though there are certainly Indian influences, as these aspects of cooking seem to be genetically juxtaposed into my genes. Sometimes it's evident as an underlying note—perhaps the soft spice of black pepper in a fruit cobbler. Sometimes it's as powerful as adding saffron to a leg of lamb. And sometimes it's as

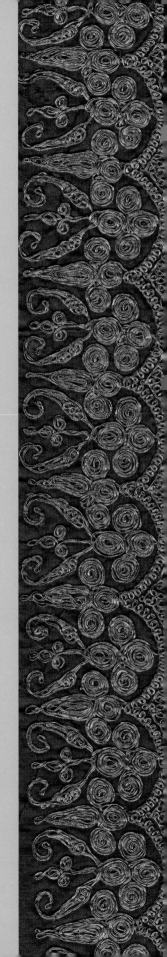

simple as gently warming rosemary and thyme in olive oil before adding them to a sauce, to coax out the herbs' dormant underlying notes. What I hope you discover is that by using commonly found spices and herbs, roots, shoots, grains, beans, and lentils, it's possible to take something ordinary, like a common chicken breast, and transform it into something amazing.

In India, we use spices as often as we can, and in as many ways as you can think of: toasted, ground, made into a paste, fried, infused into oil, and whole. Saffron gets warmed in butter to accentuate its flavor and color before using; cumin seeds are toasted and ground in a coffee grinder for a smoky, earthy essence; mustard seeds are fried in hot oil to tease out their mild, sweet, and nearly peppery nuances. The use of spice is as essential to Indian cooking as knowing how to make a good stock is essential to French cooking. Cooking with spices constitutes the foundation of Indian cuisine, involving layering flavors in simple yet profoundly effective ways. And there is no reason why these techniques can't be applied to chicken wings and meat loaf, a roast turkey or enchiladas. Using spices to their full advantage is the secret to making dishes that are already a part of your repertoire really sing.

Like you, I rely mostly on supermarket staples. And I don't expect other home cooks to go searching high and low for specialty ingredients. I always have tomatoes, red peppers, red onions, cilantro, ginger, lemons, and limes in my refrigerator, as these ingredients tend to migrate into my cooking on a daily basis. I also use kosher salt because I find it easier to control and sprinkle in by hand than table salt. Cayenne pepper, jalapeño peppers, and chile peppers are like black pepper to me and I use them as liberally, but you can decrease (or increase!) their quantities as you like. There are, however, a few ingredients that are nice to have on hand, like fenugreek leaves; fresh curry leaves (you can store them in your freezer); and spice mixes like chaat masala, garam masala, and sambhaar that stay fresh for up to six months. (I also provide recipes for the latter two spice blends.) Fenugreek leaves and chaat masala can be found in most any Indian supermarket, or simply order them from one of the resources in the back of the book on page 253. If you can't find or don't have a particular ingredient, don't stress about it—just eliminate it from the recipe. This is what cooking is about, flexibility and improvisation. Maybe you will come up with a dish even better than mine.

I find that keeping cooking easy is the only way to cook for others while still enjoying entertaining. Cooking at home should not be about drama and fuss. It should be fun. In fact, it's usually my home-cooked creations that inspire the dishes on my restaurants' menus, not vice versa. I'm proud to admit that there are those who consider themselves addicted to my style of cooking. They arrive with their Tupperware in tow (most of my dinner guests know that I usually cook enough food to feed an army) and travel far and wide to eat at my table. This does not mean that I cook elaborate, complicated restaurant-style dishes. I cook as any home cook does—with the ingredients at hand and in the simplest manner possible. I wrote *American Masala* keeping in mind how I really cook in my kitchen and have taken care to write about the shortcuts and time-saving tips I employ. My goal is to enjoy my time in the kitchen, cooking with the most beautiful, seasonal, and delicious ingredients I can find.

The recipes in this book are the ones that I make for, and share with, friends and family. They are as at home in the country as they are in the city or suburbs. You won't find recipes for traditional Indian dishes—or Italian ones or Mexican ones. Instead you'll find a delicious mix, as unique and diverse as New York City, and yet as familiar as your mother's cooking. I hope you find as much gratification from the recipes on the pages that follow as I do.

CHAPTER 1

chutneys, pickles, and spices

It is said that in the old days of India, a meal had to have at least fifty-six different and distinct tastes to be considered a good one. Chappan Bhog is the legendary tradition that culminates in a parade of every flavor combination imaginable, from floral to acrid, crisp to succulent, and hot to cold. Thankfully, this strict measure of a good meal has since relaxed, but most Indian homes still strive to create a variety of taste sensations during a meal. This is achieved through a lively assortment of sauces, condiments, pickles, and relishes. In fact, it is often not what is served as the main course or side dishes that demonstrates the culinary artistry of an Indian cook but rather the accompaniments he or she presents with the meal. As ubiquitous as mustard and ketchup, Indian pickles, raitas, chutneys, and spice blends have a great many uses. Sometimes all you need to enhance your enjoyment of a dish is a teaspoonful of chutney or a few bites of pickle.

Spice rubs and powders, while not necessarily offered at the table as a condiment, are just as important to have within reach. These blends are famous for packing a more multidimensional punch than most whole spices ever could. The assortment of raitas, chutneys, pickles, sauces, and spices in this chapter, though varied and delicious, is minute when compared to the whole world of Indian condiments. That said, it's amazing how, with just a few of these condiments tucked neatly away in your cupboard or refrigerator, you can instantly transform food.

Achaars (pickles that are either raw or cooked and left in the sun to cure), chutneys (cooked, ground, or both), murrabas (preserves), podis (spice powders), kachumbars (salads), and raitas (yogurt sauces with spices and sometimes fruit or vegetables) are all part of most every Indian cook's repertoire. Each family has its own special way of making these familiar accompaniments, and the recipes are guarded carefully and handed down from generation to generation since it is believed that when you give away the recipe for your family's pickles, you are giving away the soul of your family's cuisine.

My mother is considered the condiment expert in my family's social circle in New Delhi. She has collected pickle and chutney recipes from both sides of the family as well as from friends. These time-tested recipes, paired with her patience and respect for culture, tradition, and heritage, grant her that rarefied position. When mangoes, gooseberries, lotus stems, ginger, radishes, or tomatoes come into season, she makes massive batches of chutneys and pickles, enough to last our immediate and extended families and friends until the next harvest.

Familiar Indian essentials like Tamarind Chutney, Raita, and Garam Masala bring a taste of India to many of the dishes I cook now. Likewise, I've discovered new spices and relishes to love and depend on since coming to the United States. I first experienced Cranberry Chutney when I visited my partner Charlie's family in West Virginia for Thanksgiving. Harissa, my favorite Middle Eastern condiment, packs a ton of heat and spice in one tiny droplet. Stir a quarter teaspoon into a large bowl of hummus and taste how it evolves; drizzle a little into a dull soup and it will make it lively.

While these accompaniments may seem simple, they serve great purpose. They can uplift the easiest and fastest of meals, like a fish fillet, a pork chop, or a modest bowl of soup. Invest some time in their preparation and taste how these quick pantry items take your cooking to a whole new level of ease and flavor.

spicy harissa

MAKES ½ CUP

8 garlic cloves, unpeeled
4 ounces dried red chiles
1 tablespoon coriander seeds
1½ teaspoons cumin seeds

1½ cups water
1 cup extra-virgin olive oil
1 teaspoon kosher salt

Preheat your broiler to high. Place the garlic on a baking sheet and roast until all of its sides are deep brown, turning often, about 10 to 15 minutes. Remove the garlic from the oven. Once cool, peel and set aside.

Place the chiles, coriander seeds, and cumin seeds in a medium saucepan over medium-high heat and toast for 5 minutes (turn your hood fan on if you are sensitive to chiles; they get smoky). Add the water and cook for 2 minutes. Cover, turn off the heat, and let the chiles soak for 20 minutes.

Strain the chiles and place them in a food processor with the peeled garlic, oil, and salt. Puree until well blended and smooth. Transfer to a covered plastic container. As long as you replenish the olive oil occasionally so that there is always a thin layer on top, Harissa will keep for many weeks, and even months.

MOUSTACHE IS ONE of my favorite Middle Eastern restaurants in New York City's West Village. After much badgering, the owner gave me the recipe for his excellent Harissa. I've tinkered with it throughout the years to reflect my palate. You can use any kind of dried red chiles to make this spiced oil; I like using one part Kashmiri chiles to one part Thai chiles. Note that the heat level will decrease or increase depending on the kind of chiles you use. Harissa lasts for a long time if stored properly. Place it in a sealed jar and top it off with olive oil every time you use it to create an air-lock film above the Harissa and always use a clean spoon when dipping into the sauce.

green chutney (haree chutney)

MAKES 1½ CUPS

1 cup chopped fresh cilantro

1 cup chopped fresh mint leaves

1 green mango, peeled, fruit sliced away from the pit, and roughly chopped

2 to 3 jalapeños (cored and seeded if you prefer a milder flavor), roughly chopped

A 2-inch piece fresh ginger, peeled and cut into chunks

½ red onion, quartered

Juice of 1 lemon

1 tablespoon sugar

1 teaspoon kosher salt

Place all of the ingredients in a blender and add ¼ cup of water. Blend until smooth, scraping down the sides of the jar as needed. If the chutney doesn't blend easily, add a little more water to facilitate the process (this will make the chutney milder). Taste for seasoning, transfer to a covered plastic container, and refrigerate for up to 5 days.

GREEN CHUTNEY is made by nearly every family in northern India, where it is served with just about every meal. A mixture of mint, cilantro, and green mango, this recipe is easy to alter—you can make it solely with cilantro, you can increase the amount of chiles to make it super-hot (I've been known to add up to 10, depending on my mood), or you can make the mint stand out by increasing its proportion in relation to the cilantro (do use some cilantro or the chutney will taste bitter). It's especially lovely with foods from the grill.

CANNING

TO CAN ANY CHUTNEY, preserve, or condiment, such as Spicy Harissa (page 7) or Candied Orange Peel (page 248), follow these simple instructions:

Wash your jars and lids in hot, soapy water and rinse well. Place the jars in a large pot and cover with 2 inches of water. Bring to a boil, cover, and boil for 10 minutes. Remove the jars using tongs and place upside down on a clean kitchen towel to drain. Repeat with the lids.

Fill the jars, leaving a ¼-inch head space at the top. Wipe off the rims with a clean kitchen towel. Place the lids on the jars and seal. Place the filled jars on a rack in a very deep pot (about double the height of the jar) or canner and cover with water. Bring to a boil, cover, and boil for 10 minutes (water will probably spit out from beneath the lid). Remove the jars from the pot using tongs and place on a clean kitchen towel to cool. Leave the jars out overnight at room temperature before refrigerating.

spiced pear chutney

MAKES ABOUT 2 CUPS

3 tablespoons canola oil
3 to 6 dried red chiles
1½ teaspoons fennel seeds
1 teaspoon cumin seeds
¼ cup dried fenugreek leaves (optional)
½ teaspoon sweet paprika
Pinch of asafetida

3½ pounds (about 6) Bartlett or d'Anjou pears, peeled, cored, quartered, and thinly sliced crosswise
1½ teaspoons kosher salt
¼ cup sugar
2 tablespoons white wine vinegar

Heat the oil with the chiles, fennel seeds, and cumin seeds in a large saucepan or skillet over medium-high heat until the cumin is browned, 2 to 2½ minutes. Stir in the fenugreek leaves (if using), paprika, and asafetida and cook for 15 seconds. Add the pears and salt and cook until the pears get juicy, 3 to 4 minutes. Stir in the sugar and vinegar, reduce the heat to medium, and cook until the pears are soft, sticky, and deeply golden and caramelized, stirring often, 35 to 45 minutes. Taste for seasoning, transfer to a plastic container, and refrigerate for up to 1 week, or ladle into dry and sterilized jars and can according to the manufacturer's instructions or the instructions on page 8.

IN HIMACHAL Pradesh and Kashmir, two northern Indian states, fruit orchards are abundant, as are amazing pears. I created this recipe thinking of these regions. It has since become a classic at my restaurant in New York City. Can the chutney and offer it as hostess gifts or to friends. It is excellent with most any roasted meat, as well as on a sandwich. Fenugreek leaves add a gentle bitter contrast to the sweetness of the pears, but if you can't find dried fenugreek leaves, simply omit them.

sweet-tart cranberry chutney

MAKES 9 CUPS

1 (12-ounce) bag fresh or frozen
  cranberries
3 Granny Smith apples, peeled, cored, and
  quartered
3 blood oranges or navel oranges,
  scrubbed, quartered, and any seeds
  removed

1 pineapple, peeled, cored, and cut into
  large chunks
1 cup sugar
1 cup chopped pecans
½ cup dried strawberries
¼ cup dried cherries
¼ cup dried cranberries

Place all of the ingredients into a food processor (if your food processor is not large enough to hold all of the ingredients, then make the chutney in two batches) and pulse to combine a few times until everything is very finely chopped. Refrigerate overnight and serve the next day. Cranberry Chutney can be made up to 2 days in advance.

I WAS FIRST ENCHANTED by Mother Burd's cranberry salad at Thanksgiving. The fresh flavors are so pure and sweet that you may never make a traditional cranberry sauce again. Dried fruits lend a nice texture while pineapple offers a lovely tanginess. Though this chutney is American through and through, its spirit reminds me of the fruit chutneys that I've eaten in the Himalayan state of Himachal Pradesh, where fruits are used in a variety of savory preparations.

tamarind chutney

MAKES ABOUT 1¼ CUPS

1 tablespoon canola oil
1 teaspoon cumin seeds
1 teaspoon ground ginger
½ teaspoon cayenne pepper
½ teaspoon fennel seeds

½ teaspoon asafetida (optional)
½ teaspoon Garam Masala (page 20)
2 cups water
1¼ cups sugar
3 tablespoons tamarind concentrate

Heat the oil and spices in a medium saucepan over medium-high heat and cook until the spices are fragrant and lightly toasted, about 1 minute. Whisk in the water, sugar, and tamarind concentrate until completely dissolved and bring to a boil. Turn the heat down to medium and simmer until the sauce turns chocolaty brown and it is thick enough to leave a trail on the back of a spoon, 20 to 30 minutes. (While still warm it will look like chocolate sauce and it will thicken a bit as it cools.) Taste for seasoning, transfer to a covered plastic container, and store in the refrigerator for up to 2 weeks or ladle into dry and sterilized jars and can according to the manufacturer's instructions or the instructions on page or the instructions on page 8.

THIS IS MY PARTNER Charlie's favorite condiment. He has lived in India, traveled throughout that country extensively, and has eaten in many celebrated homes and restaurants, but this recipe remains his favorite. In fact, he often gets us both into trouble by admitting to my mother that he likes my version better than hers! You can keep this in a tightly sealed jar for several weeks if you store it carefully and always use a clean spoon (no double dipping) to take some from the jar. I use Tamarind Chutney in the recipes for Abha Aunty's Sweet-and-Sour Eggplant (page 163) as well as to glaze the Tamarind-Glazed Turkey with Corn Bread–Jalapeño Stuffing (page 142).

better-than-ketchup tomato chutney

MAKES ABOUT 3 CUPS

¼ cup canola oil

36 curry leaves, roughly torn (optional)

2 teaspoons mustard seeds

2 teaspoons cumin seeds

12 dried red chiles

½ teaspoon turmeric

3½ pounds tomatoes (about 6 or 7), cored and roughly chopped

1 (4.4-ounce) tube double-concentrated tomato paste or 1 (9-ounce) can tomato paste

2 tablespoons sugar

1½ tablespoons kosher salt

½ teaspoon cayenne pepper

1 teaspoon Sambhaar (page 21) or rasam powder, or ½ teaspoon curry powder

Heat the oil with the curry leaves (if using), mustard seeds, cumin seeds, and chiles in a large pot or skillet over medium-high heat until the cumin is browned, about 2 minutes. Add the turmeric and cook until the chiles darken, 1 to 2 minutes longer. Add the remaining ingredients and cook for 10 minutes, stirring occasionally and pressing the tomatoes against the sides of the pot to mash them if they are not breaking up on their own. Reduce the heat to medium and cook until the chutney is thick and jammy (if canning, cook until the mixture is very thick), stirring often, an additional 20 to 35 minutes. If you are using hard winter tomatoes, the chutney may cook in less time, as there is less tomato juice to reduce. Taste for seasoning, transfer to a covered plastic container, and refrigerate for up to 1 week or ladle into dry and sterilized jars and can according to the manufacturer's instructions or the instructions on page 8.

RAQUEL'S HUSBAND, Matt, eats this chutney like it's going out of style. Sometimes I have to remind him that it's a condiment and not a side dish! He slathers it on omelets, eats it with steak and even with cheese and crackers. Lucky for Matt that Tomato Chutney can be made year round with either summer-ripe or winter-pale tomatoes. I will be forever indebted to my friend Durga's mother, a neighbor in New Delhi, who introduced me to Tomato Chutney, and who is originally from Hyderabad, the pickling capital of the south. She got me hooked on it from a very young age.

toasted cumin

MAKES ABOUT ½ CUP

½ **cup cumin seeds**

Place cumin seeds in a large skillet over medium-high heat. Toast, while shaking the skillet occasionally, until the cumin becomes a toasty brown color and starts to smoke, 4 to 5 minutes. Place the cumin seeds in a bowl to cool. Once cooled, grind in a spice grinder or coffee mill until powder fine. Store in an airtight container for up to 4 months.

TOASTING CUMIN SEEDS and grinding them powder fine is one of my favorite spice tricks. The smell and taste of toasted cumin is unbelievable. Besides adding it to stir-fries, I like to add a pinch to guacamole and fresh salsas.

ginger-pickled onions

MAKES ABOUT 2 CUPS

1 large red onion, halved and sliced into thin wedges

A 1-inch piece fresh ginger, peeled and sliced into thin sticks

½ jalapeño, halved

Juice of 1 lemon

Rice vinegar

Place the onion, ginger, and jalapeño in a plastic container that has a tight-fitting lid. Add the lemon juice and enough vinegar to completely submerge the onion. Cover the container and refrigerate for at least 1 day before using. The pickles can be refrigerated for up to 1 week, but note that they will lose their crispness the longer they age.

THIS IS ONE of the easiest Indian pickles to make. Here the addition of ginger and jalapeño makes it extra fancy. It's delicious as a side to grilled meat or dal or when used as an ingredient in a salad like Avocado Salad (page 54). The onions turn a shocking magenta after resting in the vinegar for a day and reach their absolute flavor zenith 2 to 3 days after making.

raita

1 (32-ounce) container plain yogurt

1 medium tomato, finely chopped, or 1 cup of one of the ingredients mentioned below

1 medium red onion, finely minced, or 1 cup of one of the ingredients mentioned below

1 cup roughly chopped fresh cilantro, or ½ cup chopped fresh cilantro and ½ cup chopped fresh mint leaves

½ jalapeño (cored and seeded if you prefer a milder flavor), finely diced (optional)

2 teaspoons Toasted Cumin (page 16)

2 teaspoons sugar

1½ teaspoons kosher salt

1 teaspoon chaat masala (optional)

½ teaspoon ground peppercorns

⅛ teaspoon cayenne pepper

Mix all of the ingredients in a large bowl and serve immediately or refrigerate in a covered plastic container for up to 4 days.

ON THE INDIAN TABLE raita is a beloved condiment whose ingredients change according to the season, function, and meal. It's eaten not only for its cooling effect, which makes it great with spicy dishes but also for its healthful bacteria, protein, and calcium content. This is a basic recipe that you can alter as you like. Add or subtract ingredients like grated cucumbers, grated zucchini and summer squash, halved grapes, pineapple chunks, whole chickpeas, chopped boiled potatoes, chopped mangoes, raw sweet corn, and minced shallots. If the cilantro you are using has thick stems that crack when snapped off, be sure to remove them. If the stems are thin and delicate, you don't need to worry about carefully separating the leaves from the stems.

garam masala

MAKES ABOUT ¾ CUP

1 tablespoon dried miniature rosebuds
(optional)
A 1-inch piece cinnamon stick, broken
into pieces
2 bay leaves
¼ cup cumin seeds
⅓ cup coriander seeds

1 tablespoon green cardamom pods
1 tablespoon whole black peppercorns
2 teaspoons whole cloves
1 dried red chile
¼ teaspoon freshly grated nutmeg
⅛ teaspoon ground mace

If the roses have stems, break them off and discard. Heat the roses with the cinnamon, bay leaves, cumin seeds, coriander seeds, cardamom pods, whole peppercorns, cloves, and chile in a medium skillet over medium-high heat, stirring often, until the cumin becomes brown, 2½ to 3 minutes. Transfer to a spice grinder or coffee mill, add the nutmeg and mace, and grind until powder fine. Store in an airtight container for up to 4 months.

GARAM MASALA is the Indian equivalent of French herbes de Provence or Chinese five-spice powder. The recipe changes from region to region within northern India and can be varied according to whim. Here, rosebuds (found in Indian or Middle Eastern markets) add an exciting floral note, but you can substitute black cardamom, fennel seeds (in the style of Kashmir), or a teaspoon of royal cumin (shahi or kala zeera, also found in Indian markets)—or just eliminate the roses altogether. Once you taste the difference that this simple powder makes in your cooking, you will find it worth the investment of cupboard space. As a rule (one that certainly gets broken at times), Garam Masala is only added at the last step of cooking, almost like a fresh herb, because it tends to become bitter if cooked too long.

sambhaar

MAKES ABOUT 3/4 CUP

3 dried red chiles
2 tablespoons coriander seeds
2 tablespoons mustard seeds
1 tablespoon cumin seeds
1 tablespoon white lentils (urad dal)

1 tablespoon yellow split peas
  (channa dal)
2 teaspoons fenugreek seeds
2 teaspoons ground peppercorns
40 curry leaves (optional)

Place all of the spices in a medium skillet over medium-high heat. Toast until the mustard seeds begin to pop and the skillet starts to smoke, stirring often, 3^1/$_2$ to 5 minutes. Transfer to a spice grinder or coffee mill and grind until powder fine. Store in an airtight glass jar for up to 4 months.

SAMBHAAR IS A SPICE BLEND that is the southern Indian equivalent to Garam Masala, a spice blend used often in northern India. The nutty flavor comes from the addition of channa dal (yellow split peas) and urad dal (small white lentils). I don't add the customary amount of fenugreek seeds as they can make the Sambhaar overwhelmingly bitter; if you crave a more traditional flavor, then double the amount of fenugreek. Add Sambhaar to soups, stews, and sauces or sprinkle onto meat before broiling or grilling.

CHAPTER 2

snacks and starters

I never give my mom enough credit for teaching me how to cook. Once I was old enough to see over the countertop (and just barely at that), I fell under the spell of Panditji, my family's much fabled, exalted, and talented chef of sixty-odd years. He engineered magic in the kitchen, creating the most exotic aromas and exciting marriages of flavors and textures. As a child, it was easy to get caught up in Panditji's culinary alchemy.

But when my family left the city in the summer for cooler locales, or when Panditji was on vacation, Mom took over the kitchen. She entertained my father's colleagues with elaborate dinner parties and cooked endless snacks and meals for me, my brother and sister, and all of our friends after rigorous games of cricket or lazy afternoons of doing nothing at all. Now, living many seas away from New Delhi, I find myself turning to Mom's style of cooking more and more. Mom cooks sensibly, practically, and without fuss or drama. She is the queen of keeping things simple. This is what I hope that these recipes encourage you to do—to be a clever cook, using pantry ingredients to create imaginative and boldly delicious snacks and appetizers that are easy to prepare and are satisfying beyond expectations.

The restaurant culture in India is still very young, and more often than not, the best food you can experience in the country comes from a home kitchen. In India, and at my tiny New York apartment, unexpected drop-in guests are expected, and it's smart to have staples like red onions, red bell peppers, potatoes, and jalapeños, the founding ingredients of many dishes, ready to be turned into a substantial snack dish at a moment's notice. With fresh or day-old bread, defrosted shrimp, and canned tomatoes

I can make spicy Shrimp Balchao Bruschetta. With whatever wedges I might find in the refrigerator cheese drawer, like Taleggio, aged Cheddar, Gouda, or Fontina, I can make Three-Cheese Spinach Dip, Quesadillas with Pico de Gallo, and Mushroom and Taleggio Turnovers (it's always handy to have a box of puff pastry in the freezer). Sometimes I have nothing more than a couple of potatoes in the house. On these occasions, I turn the humblest of ingredients into the delightful Aloo Bonda Potato Dumplings.

This chapter is a reflection of what I learned from Mom. Most of the recipes that follow can be prepared last minute, as she usually did, though no one will ever guess it. As you cook from these pages, you will find nothing too tedious. It may sometimes be a little less familiar, for there are probably some cultural nuances that may not have been a part of your upbringing, but I encourage you to try them, taste them, and make them your own.

three-cheese spinach dip

SERVES 8 TO 10

FOR THE DIP

1 pound frozen spinach, thawed

4 tablespoons (½ stick) unsalted butter

½ teaspoon ground peppercorns

¼ teaspoon red pepper flakes

¼ teaspoon dried thyme

2 tablespoons all-purpose flour

2 cups heavy cream

4 ounces aged Gouda cheese, grated

4 ounces Parmigiano-Reggiano cheese,
  grated

⅛ teaspoon freshly grated nutmeg

1 teaspoon kosher salt

FOR THE TOPPING

8 ounces Fontina cheese, grated

¼ cup panko bread crumbs

¼ teaspoon ground peppercorns

Tortilla chips or a bread bowl, for serving

To make the dip, wrap the spinach in a clean kitchen towel and wring until the spinach is free of liquid. Melt the butter with the ground peppercorns, pepper flakes, and thyme in a large saucepan over medium-high heat, cooking until fragrant, about 1½ minutes. Add the flour, reduce the heat to medium, and stir for 1½ minutes. Whisk in the heavy cream and cook until the mixture begins to thicken and bubble, stirring occasionally, 2 to 3 minutes. Stir in the Gouda and Parmigiano-Reggiano cheeses, spinach, nutmeg, and salt and continue cooking for 2 minutes. Transfer the spinach mixture to a shallow 1½-quart oven-safe casserole or gratin dish. (At this point the dip can be refrigerated for up to 2 days; bring to room temperature before proceeding.)

Set an oven rack 6 inches from the heating element and preheat the broiler. Make the topping: Combine the topping ingredients and sprinkle over the spinach dip. Broil until the cheese is browned and bubbly, 5 to 10 minutes (watch carefully as broilers vary). Serve with tortilla chips or a bread bowl.

THIS SPINACH DIP may be the richest, creamiest, and most satisfying that you have ever made. It's redolent with heady cheeses like Parmigiano-Reggiano and Gouda and emerges from the oven with a golden Fontina crust. If you plan on serving the dip in a bread bowl, brush the edges of the hollowed-out bread with olive oil or melted butter prior to placing it under the broiler—and keep an eye on the bread to make sure it doesn't burn while the cheese browns (you can cover the edge with a ring of aluminum foil to protect it).

toasted garlic hummus

SERVES 8 TO 10

2 garlic cloves
2 (15-ounce) cans chickpeas, drained and
    rinsed, or 1½ cups dried chickpeas,
    soaked overnight and boiled until
    tender
½ cup water
¼ cup extra-virgin olive oil
Juice of 1½ lemons plus ½ lemon, cut
    into wedges, for serving

½ teaspoon Toasted Cumin (page 16;
    optional)
¼ teaspoon Aleppo pepper (optional)
2½ teaspoons kosher salt
¼ teaspoon ground peppercorns
⅓ cup tahini
Ground sumac, for sprinkling (optional)
Pita bread, for serving

Preheat the broiler. Place the garlic on a baking sheet and broil until all of its sides are browned and the garlic is soft, turning often, 8 to 12 minutes. Remove the garlic from the oven, cool, and then peel and coarsely chop.

Using a food processor, pulse together the garlic, all but 1 tablespoon of the chickpeas, the water, oil, lemon juice, Toasted Cumin (if using), Aleppo pepper, salt, and ground peppercorns until the mixture is smooth. Scrape down the sides of the bowl as needed. Add the tahini and blend for 2 minutes (if you like fluffy Hummus, process it for a couple of extra minutes). Taste and adjust the salt and lemon juice if necessary and serve sprinkled with the reserved chickpeas and a pinch of sumac (if desired). Serve with lemon wedges and plenty of pita bread.

FOR TRULY AMAZING HUMMUS, soak dried chickpeas overnight and then cook them in fresh water until tender, about 1¼ to 1½ hours the following day. The resulting hummus has a silkier texture than that made with canned chickpeas. If you use a dark brown, deeply roasted tahini, your hummus may need extra lemon juice; the converse is true if you use a pale, more delicate tahini.

guacamole with toasted cumin

SERVES 8 TO 10

4 avocados, halved, pitted, and chopped
1 tomato, diced
1 small red onion, diced
½ cup chopped fresh cilantro
1 jalapeño (cored and seeded if you prefer
  a milder flavor), finely chopped

2 teaspoons kosher salt
½ teaspoon ground peppercorns
⅛ teaspoon Toasted Cumin (page 16)
Juice of 2 limes
Tortilla chips, for serving

Place the avocados in a large bowl. Add the tomato, onion, cilantro, jalapeño, salt, ground peppercorns, Toasted Cumin, and lime juice. Combine with a large spoon. Taste and adjust salt if necessary; serve with tortilla chips.

IT WASN'T UNTIL I was twenty-three years old that I fell in love with avocados. While staying at my friend Ruth Leserman's home in Beverly Hills, I experienced them plucked fresh off the tree, sliced, and slathered on toast with just a sprinkle of salt and pepper as garnish. From that day on, avocados—especially in guacamole—became one of my favorite foods. Toasted Cumin adds a beautiful nuanced and savory quality to the guacamole. For an extra smoky flavor, char the jalapeño over an open flame prior to chopping.

warm roasted pepper dip

SERVES 8 TO 10

3 tablespoons canola oil

1 small red onion, roughly chopped

4 large red bell peppers, cored, seeded, and roughly chopped

2 medium tomatoes, cored and sliced into thick wedges

4 garlic cloves, peeled

1 jalapeño (cored and seeded if you prefer a milder flavor)

1 teaspoon kosher salt

½ teaspoon ground peppercorns

¼ cup heavy cream (more if you like a thinner dip)

¼ pound mozzarella or queso fresco, cut into small cubes

Tortilla chips, for serving

Preheat your oven to 450°F. Grease a large glass baking dish with 1 tablespoon of the oil. Add the onion, bell peppers, tomatoes, garlic, and jalapeño to the baking dish. Sprinkle with the salt and ground peppercorns, drizzle with the remaining 2 tablespoons of oil, and toss to coat. Roast the vegetables until they are soft and brown, about 1 hour, stirring every 15 minutes.

Transfer the vegetables to a blender along with the cream and process until smooth. Pour the puree into a medium saucepan and bring it to a simmer. Reduce the heat to medium, add the cheese, and cook until it starts to melt, 1 to 2 minutes. Turn off the heat. Taste and adjust the salt if necessary and serve with tortilla chips.

ONE WINTRY, SNOWY Sunday afternoon, I found myself craving something warm and comforting to snack on. A pantry and refrigerator raid produced only a couple of red bell peppers, garlic, a jalapeño, and a lonely onion. A trip to the neighborhood bodega, the small independently owned convenience stores peppered throughout New York City, proved equally uninspiring, yielding only a few rock-hard winter tomatoes and a block of mozzarella cheese. Little did I know how delicious the results of my experiment would be, for even the saddest winter vegetables take on a new identity after roasting in the oven. Warm Roasted Pepper Dip has since become one of my favorite party dips. It's also the sauce for my enchiladas (page 95.)

mushroom and taleggio turnovers

MAKES 16 TURNOVERS

4 tablespoons (½ stick) unsalted butter
1 teaspoon finely chopped fresh rosemary
¼ teaspoon red pepper flakes
½ teaspoon ground peppercorns
1 small red onion, finely chopped
2 tablespoons fruity white wine or
  vermouth
1½ pounds cremini mushrooms, trimmed
  and sliced

1 teaspoon kosher salt plus a pinch, for
  the egg wash
1 teaspoon chopped fresh thyme
1 large egg
1 tablespoon water
⅛ teaspoon cayenne pepper
All-purpose flour, for rolling pastry
2 packages frozen puff pastry, thawed
2 ounces Taleggio cheese, cut into
  16 small pieces

Melt the butter with the rosemary, pepper flakes, and ground peppercorns in a large skillet over medium-high heat, cooking until it's fragrant, about 1 minute. Add the onion, reduce the heat to medium, and cook until browned and sticky, stirring often, 5 to 7 minutes. Pour in the wine and cook 1 minute longer while scraping the onion and any browned bits off the bottom of the skillet. Add the mushrooms and cook until they release their liquid and that liquid mostly evaporates, stirring occasionally, another 5 to 7 minutes. Reduce the heat to medium-low, add the salt, and cook for an additional 10 minutes, stirring often to prevent burning (reduce heat to low if mushrooms begin to brown too much). Stir in the thyme, transfer the mushrooms to a bowl to cool, or refrigerate overnight.

Preheat the oven to 400°F. Whisk together the egg, water, cayenne pepper, and salt and set aside. Dust your work surface with flour and place 1 sheet of puff pastry on top (if it came folded in thirds, keep folded). Roll the folded pastry sheet to an approximate 13 x 8-inch rectangle. Starting 1 inch from the left edge, place a heaping 1½ tablespoons of mushrooms in the center of the pastry. Repeat three times, working your way across the pastry, leaving about 1½ inches between mounds and ending about 1 inch from the right edge. Place 1 piece of cheese on top of each mound.

Using a pastry brush, lightly paint the long edge of pastry closest to you with the egg wash. Paint the left and right edges up to the midpoint of the pastry, and then paint between each of the mounds up to the middle of the pastry. Fold the top half of the pastry down over the bottom half, press the edges together to seal, and press the dough together in between each of the mounds. Trim the edges and cut between each mound so you have 4 turnovers. Press the tines of an upturned fork around the turnovers' edges to crimp. Brush with egg wash and place on a baking sheet. Proceed with the remaining pastry and filling, making 12 more turnovers. (The turnovers can be frozen on a baking sheet until they are hard, about 1 hour, and then transferred to a large resealable plastic bag and kept frozen for up to 3 months. Let turnovers thaw before baking.) Bake the turnovers until golden brown, 15 to 20 minutes, rotating midway through cooking. Cool 10 minutes, and serve warm or at room temperature.

VARIATION: Red Pepper and Chèvre Turnovers

Substitute 1$^1/_2$ pounds diced red bell peppers for the mushrooms, cooking until they are completely softened, 6 to 8 minutes. Proceed with recipe for Mushroom and Taleggio Turnovers as instructed, substituting 2 ounces of goat cheese crumbled or sliced into 16 pieces for the Taleggio cheese.

KEEP A LARGE plastic bag of these turnovers in your freezer to serve to company. Defrost as many as you need at room temperature for an hour or two and then bake. Place the Taleggio in the freezer to ease slicing. If you can't find Taleggio, substitute any soft, melting cheese, like Fontina or Gouda.

quesadillas with pico de gallo

MAKES 4 QUESADILLAS

FOR THE PICO DE GALLO

3 medium tomatoes, cored and finely
    chopped
1 small red onion, finely chopped
2 jalapeños (cored and seeded if you
    prefer a milder flavor), finely diced
1/2 cup chopped fresh cilantro
Juice of 2 limes
1 1/4 teaspoons kosher salt
1/2 teaspoon Toasted Cumin (page 16)
1/4 teaspoon ground peppercorns

FOR THE QUESADILLAS

4 tablespoons (1/2 stick) unsalted butter,
    melted
8 (6-inch) whole-wheat tortillas (if you can
    find only 8-inch tortillas, increase the
    cheese to 1/2 cup and increase the Pico
    de Gallo to 4 tablespoons per quesadilla)
1 cup shredded cheese (any combination
    of Cheddar, mozzarella, queso blanco,
    or Monterey Jack)
Sour cream and Guacamole (page 28), for
    serving (optional)

To make the Pico de Gallo, mix all the ingredients in a large bowl. Let them stand for at least 30 minutes, or up to 24 hours, to allow the flavors to come together. Taste and adjust the seasoning as you like. Using a slotted spoon, transfer 3/4 cup Pico de Gallo to a small bowl, pressing extra liquid from the salsa with the back of a spoon, and set aside.

Preheat the oven to 200°F and place the melted butter and a pastry brush next to your stovetop. To make the quesadillas, brush one side of the tortillas with melted butter. Warm a griddle or medium nonstick skillet for 2 minutes over high heat. Reduce the heat to medium and place 1 tortilla, buttered side down, on the griddle. Sprinkle with 1/4 cup cheese. Top with 3 tablespoons strained Pico de Gallo, cover with another tortilla, and brush the top with melted butter. Cook until the tortilla is browned, about 2 minutes, and then flip. Brush the top with more melted butter and cook until the bottom is browned, 1 to 1 1/2 minutes. Flip again, cooking for 1 minute longer to brown the butter. Remove the quesadilla from the griddle. Transfer to a baking sheet and place it in the oven to stay warm. Repeat with the remaining tortillas, cheese, and salsa. To serve, cut the quesadilla into quarters and serve with the reserved Pico de Gallo, sour cream, and Guacamole.

I USED TO EAT these nearly every night with my aunt Aruna in San Francisco. She always used whole-wheat tortillas, which gave the quesadillas a chapati-like flavor. Quesadillas are incomplete without Pico de Gallo, my favorite condiment from the Mexican kitchen. Toasted Cumin enhances the savory quality of the salsa and complements the earthy quality of the whole-wheat tortillas. You can make the Pico de Gallo up to a day in advance; however, it will have to be semidrained (a slotted spoon works well) prior to serving, as it gets increasingly juicy the longer it sits.

aloo bonda potato dumplings

MAKES 20 DUMPLINGS

FOR THE FILLING

2 pounds (about 5 medium) red potatoes,
   peeled and quartered
½ teaspoon turmeric
1 tablespoon plus 1½ teaspoons kosher
   salt
1½ tablespoons canola oil
2 teaspoons mustard seeds
24 curry leaves
3 to 6 dried red chiles, coarsely crushed
A 1-inch piece fresh ginger, peeled and
   minced
1 small jalapeño (cored and seeded if you
   prefer a milder flavor), finely diced
Juice of ½ lime

FOR THE BATTER

4 cups canola oil, for frying
1 cup chickpea flour (besan)
¼ to ½ teaspoon cayenne pepper
1 teaspoon kosher salt
¼ teaspoon asafetida (optional)
½ cup water

Tomato Chutney (page 14) or ketchup

To make the filling, bring a large pot of water to a boil. Add the potatoes, turmeric, and 1 table-spoon of the salt. Reduce the heat to a simmer, cover, and cook until the potatoes are tender but not falling apart, about 25 minutes. Drain, transfer to a large bowl, and set aside.

Heat the oil, mustard seeds, and curry leaves in a large skillet over medium-high heat until the mustard seeds begin to pop, about 1½ minutes. Add the chiles and cook until the curry leaves become brittle, about 1 minute longer. Stir in the ginger and jalapeño, cooking for 30 seconds, and then add the mixture to the potatoes.

Mash the potatoes against the sides of the bowl until they are semismooth. Stir in the remaining 1½ teaspoons salt and the lime juice. Take 2 tablespoons of potato mixture and roll into a small ball, set the ball on a baking sheet, and repeat with the remaining potato mixture.

Heat the canola oil to 350°F in a medium saucepan. To make the batter, whisk together the chickpea flour, cayenne pepper, salt, and asafetida (if using) in a small bowl. Whisk in enough water so it resembles a thick pancake batter. Dip each potato ball in the batter and roll it in your hands to coat evenly. Gently drop a few battered balls into the hot oil and fry until they are golden brown, turning often, for 3 to 5 minutes. Transfer the dumplings to a paper towel–lined plate and serve hot with Tomato Chutney or ketchup.

THESE DUMPLINGS are from the Maharashtra state in India, where people love very spicy foods. Though they are often eaten for breakfast, I usually ate Aloo Bonda as an after-school snack while I was living with my family in Nagpur in western India. Made from spiced mashed potatoes that are formed into balls and dipped into chickpea flour batter and then fried, Aloo Bondas are amazing served with Tomato Chutney or ketchup. In Mumbai, you get them as street food smashed between two slices of bread with hot green chile and garlic chutney. Nandini, a dear friend from southern India and now a consummate New Yorker, makes Aloo Bondas in advance and freezes them. She microwaves them alongside a glass of water to keep them moist. Be sure to save some of the filling to make Bread Roll Fritters (page 38).

bread roll fritters

MAKES 16 FRITTERS

4 cups canola oil
16 slices sandwich bread, crusts
    removed

1 recipe Aloo Bonda Potato Dumplings
    (page 36) filling rolled into 16
    (2-tablespoon) balls
Tomato Chutney (page 14) or ketchup

Heat the canola oil to 350°F in a medium saucepan. Meanwhile, make the bread rolls. Fill a shallow pan with water and quickly dip both sides of a piece of bread in the water. Press the bread firmly between your hands to extract as much water as possible, leaving you with a pliable (but not disintegrating) piece of bread. Hold the bread slice flat and on a diagonal in the palm of your hand so it looks like a diamond. Place a potato ball in the center of the bread and form it into a long torpedo shape by cupping your hands around it and pressing the bread around the potato, making sure to enclose all of the potato within the bread.

Fry a few fritters at a time until they are golden brown, turning and basting often, about 2 to 4 minutes. Transfer to a paper towel–lined plate and serve while hot with Tomato Chutney or ketchup.

VARIATION: Bread Fritter Sandwiches

Smash 2 Aloo Bonda potato balls between 2 slices of bread, making a sandwich. Cut the sandwich in half on a diagonal. To the chickpea flour batter add $1/4$ cup chopped cilantro, $1/2$ small and finely chopped red onion, and a finely chopped jalapeño. Dip each sandwich half in the chickpea batter and fry. Serve with Tomato Chutney or ketchup.

INDIANS HAVE MASTERED the art of serving starch with starch. Take Bread Roll Fritters—a piece of soft bread wrapped around the filling from Aloo Bonda Potato Dumplings and fried until crisp and nutty. Make a full recipe of the Aloo Bonda filling and divide it in half, using some for Aloo Bond Potato Dumplings and some for Bread Roll Fritters. You can even make these with leftover Mashed Potatoes with Mustard Oil, Cilantro, and Onions (page 175).

indian eggplant caponata

MAKES 2 CUPS

2 large eggplants

1 cup water

3 tablespoons canola oil

1 large red onion, finely chopped

½ jalapeño (cored and seeded if you prefer a milder flavor), chopped

1 tablespoon kosher salt

3 garlic cloves, peeled and finely minced

1½ teaspoons ground coriander

1 teaspoon Toasted Cumin (page 16)

1 large tomato, cored and chopped

¼ cup chopped fresh cilantro

Juice of ½ lemon

Pita or bread, for serving

Set an oven rack 6 inches from the heating element and preheat the broiler. Prick the eggplants three times with the tines of a fork and place them on an aluminum foil–lined baking sheet. Char the eggplants under the broiler until they're blistered and blackened on all sides and completely deflated, 15 to 20 minutes, turning every 3 to 4 minutes. Carefully transfer the eggplant to a plate and set aside to cool. Cut the eggplant open and scrape the soft flesh from the charred skin. Transfer it to a cutting board and finely chop.

Place the cup of water next to your stovetop. Heat the canola oil in a large skillet over medium-high heat. Add the onion, jalapeño, and salt and cook until the onion is deeply browned, stirring often, for about 10 minutes. When the onion starts sticking to the bottom of the skillet, splash it with a little water and scrape up the browned bits (you may not use the entire cup of water). Reduce the heat to medium, add the garlic, and cook until fragrant, about 1 minute. Add the chopped eggplant and cook for 2 minutes, stirring occasionally. Stir in the coriander and Toasted Cumin and cook for 2 minutes. Add the tomatoes and cook until they just barely melt into the eggplant, 4 to 5 minutes (less time for ripe tomatoes). Stir in the chopped cilantro and taste for seasoning. Add the lemon juice and serve warm or cold with pita.

CHARRING EGGPLANT is a technique used widely throughout northern India. It makes sense when you think of northern India's proximity to the Middle East and that region's delectable eggplant salads and baba ghanouj. You can use an outdoor grill to char the eggplant, broil it, or use a stovetop roaster. Be persistent in turning the eggplant often so it chars evenly; the best, most intense and smoky flavor of the eggplant comes from the portion of the eggplant closest to the charred skin. If you get some charred bits in the eggplant mixture, it's okay—it adds a beautiful flecked appearance as well as a deep flavor to the caponata. I use this recipe as the base for Indian Shirred Eggs with Eggplant (page 213).

shrimp balchao bruschetta

SERVES 8

FOR THE SHRIMP
1 pound medium shrimp, peeled and
   deveined
Juice of 1 lemon or lime
2 teaspoons kosher salt
½ teaspoon ground peppercorns
½ teaspoon cayenne pepper

FOR THE SAUCE
¼ cup water
3 tablespoons canola oil
12 curry leaves, roughly torn (optional)

3 to 6 dried red chiles (optional)
1½ teaspoons cumin seeds
¼ teaspoon ground peppercorns
2 red onions, chopped
2 teaspoons kosher salt
1 tablespoon sugar
1 tablespoon white wine vinegar
1½ cups canned chopped tomatoes
1 tablespoon unsalted butter
4 slices of bread, preferably brioche,
   brushed with melted butter, toasted,
   and halved diagonally

To prepare the shrimp, place them in a gallon-sized resealable plastic bag. Add the lemon or lime juice, salt, ground peppercorns, and cayenne pepper, shake to coat, and refrigerate while you prepare the sauce.

To make the sauce, place the water next to your stovetop. Heat the canola oil, curry leaves (if using), chiles (if using), cumin seeds, and ground peppercorns in a large saucepan over medium-high heat until the cumin browns, about 2 minutes. Add the onions and salt and cook until they're browned and sticky, 7 to 10 minutes. When the onions start sticking to the bottom of the pan, splash with water and stir and scrape up the browned bits. Stir in the sugar and vinegar and cook for 1 minute. Add the tomatoes and cook until the texture of the sauce is thick and jammy, about 4 minutes. Add the butter and once it has melted, remove the shrimp from the marinade and add them to the saucepan, cooking until they are curled and opaque, 2 to 4 minutes. Place 3 or 4 shrimp on each toast, spoon some sauce over the top, and serve.

PORTUGAL ONCE GOVERNED GOA, and like many Goan recipes this one is heavily influenced by Portuguese ingredients like vinegar and bread. The cayenne pepper and dried red chile peppers are optional—omit them completely if you prefer a milder flavor, or, for a truly authentic Goan taste, add more. Shrimp Balchao is extra indulgent on buttered brioche toasts. For passed hors d'oeuvres, chop the shrimp into bite-sized pieces. For a main course that serves three or four people, forget the bread and serve the shrimp with rice.

sweet pepper, onion, and chèvre bruschetta

MAKES 8 PIECES

3 tablespoons extra-virgin olive oil

1 tablespoon unsalted butter

1 teaspoon chopped fresh rosemary

1/2 teaspoon ground peppercorns

1 medium red onion, sliced

3 garlic cloves, peeled and smashed

2 teaspoons kosher salt

3 large red bell peppers, cored, seeded, and thinly sliced lengthwise, or 3 jarred roasted red peppers

2 small tomatoes, cored, seeded, and sliced into thin strips lengthwise

1 1/2 tablespoons capers (rinsed if salt packed)

1 teaspoon good-quality aged balsamic vinegar

6 ounces log-shaped chèvre, sliced into 8 medium-thick rounds

8 thick slices country bread, both sides brushed with olive oil and toasted

Heat the oil, butter, rosemary, and ground peppercorns in a large skillet over medium-high heat, cooking until the butter melts, about 1 minute. Stir in the onion and cook until browned and sticky, stirring often, about 5 minutes. Add the garlic and salt and cook until the garlic becomes fragrant, about 1 minute longer. Stir in the peppers and cook for 4 minutes. Reduce the heat to medium, cover, and cook for 5 minutes. Turn off the heat and let the vegetables rest for 10 minutes.

Remove the cover and increase the heat to medium-high, stirring occasionally for 3 minutes. Add the tomatoes and capers and cook until the tomatoes melt into the peppers, about 5 minutes. Turn off the heat. Stir in the vinegar, taste and adjust salt if necessary, and set aside to cool.

Set an oven rack so it is 6 inches from the heating element and preheat the broiler. Top each bread slice with some of the pepper mixture and cover with a round of goat cheese. Broil until the cheese is warmed and just beginning to brown, 3 to 6 minutes (watch the toasts closely as broilers vary). Transfer to a platter and serve warm.

I DISCOVERED THE SECRET to making peppers silky and tender purely by accident. I was making this recipe and couldn't find the matching lid to my skillet, so I used a lid one size too small. It suctioned itself onto the skillet, and it took me 10 minutes to figure out how to pry it off! The 10-minute rest gave the peppers enough time to plump and has become one of my most fortunate mistakes. Great goat cheese makes all the difference in this recipe. Angela Miller makes a beautiful chèvre at her Vermont-based Consider Bardwell farm, where fresh Oberhasli goat's milk is hand ladled to make the creamiest fresh goat's milk cheeses you could imagine.

manchurian chicken

SERVES 8

4¼ teaspoons kosher salt
2½ teaspoons ground peppercorns
1½ teaspoons cayenne pepper
1½ pounds boneless, skinless chicken breasts, sliced crosswise into 1-inch strips

Canola oil
⅓ cup cornstarch
2 large eggs
8 garlic cloves, peeled and finely chopped
1½ cups ketchup

Mix 2 teaspoons salt, 1 teaspoon ground peppercorns, and ½ teaspoon cayenne pepper in a gallon-sized resealable plastic bag. Add the chicken and turn to coat. Refrigerate for 30 minutes or up to 3 hours.

Heat 2 inches of canola oil a large saucepan until it reaches 350°F. Whisk the cornstarch, 2 teaspoons salt, 1 teaspoon ground peppercorns, ½ teaspoon cayenne pepper, and the eggs in a large bowl. Dip the chicken in the batter and then fry in small batches until golden brown, turning often, for about 5 minutes. Transfer to a paper towel–lined plate and set aside.

Heat 2 tablespoons canola oil and the remaining ½ teaspoon ground peppercorns in a large skillet over medium-high heat for 1 minute. Add the garlic and cook until it is fragrant, about 1 minute, stirring often. Add the ketchup and cook for 2 minutes, stirring occasionally. Reduce the heat to medium and add the remaining ½ teaspoon cayenne pepper and ¼ teaspoon salt. Cook until the ketchup thickens and becomes thick and deep red in color, stirring occasionally, 6 to 8 minutes. Add the fried chicken strips to the sauce and stir to coat evenly. Simmer together for 2 minutes and then serve.

THIS IS PART of a repertoire of recipes that have come to be synonymous with Indian-Chinese cookery. Manchurian is the name for dishes made with crispy vegetables or proteins that are then tossed in a sweet-and-sour ketchup-based sauce. Instead of substituting cornstarch for some of the ketchup as do many restaurants in India (with the unfortunate result of a gloppy sauce), I reduce the sauce into a thick, satiny consistency that clings to the chicken. This also can be served as a main course for two or three people.

crab-and-salmon cakes with spicy cilantro aïoli

MAKES 12 SMALL CAKES

FOR THE AÏOLI

⅔ cup mayonnaise

½ cup chopped fresh cilantro

1 jalapeño (cored and seeded if you prefer a milder flavor), finely chopped

A ½-inch piece fresh ginger, peeled and finely chopped

Juice of ½ lemon

FOR THE CAKES

1 salmon fillet (about 8 ounces), any bones removed with tweezers

1 tablespoon plus 1½ teaspoons kosher salt

1 teaspoon ground peppercorns

Juice of ½ lemon

1 pound (about 2 large) russet potatoes, peeled and chopped

Canola oil

1 teaspoon black mustard seeds

8 ounces lump crabmeat, picked over for any bits of shell or cartilage

½ cup chopped fresh cilantro

A ½-inch piece ginger, peeled and finely chopped

1 jalapeño (cored and seeded if you prefer a milder flavor), finely chopped

2 large eggs

2 tablespoons water

½ cup all-purpose flour

1¼ cups panko bread crumbs

To make the aïoli, mix all of the ingredients in a small bowl. Cover with plastic wrap and refrigerate while you make the salmon and crab cakes.

Preheat your oven to 450°F. To prepare the cakes, sprinkle the flesh side of the salmon with ½ teaspoon salt, ¼ teaspoon ground peppercorns, and half of the lemon juice. Line a baking sheet with aluminum foil and place the fish on top, skin side up. Bake until the salmon is firm and opaque at its center, 10 to 15 minutes. Once cool, peel off the skin and break the salmon into large, flaky pieces.

Boil the potatoes with 2 teaspoons salt until they're tender, 10 to 15 minutes. Drain, transfer to a large bowl, and mash with a fork or potato masher.

Heat 2 teaspoons of the oil with the mustard seeds in a small saucepan over medium-high heat, cooking until the mustard seeds start to pop, 1½ to 2 minutes. Pour the mustard seeds and the oil over the potatoes. Add the salmon, crabmeat, cilantro, ginger, jalapeño, 1½ teaspoons salt, and ½ teaspoon of the ground peppercorns and mix together. Shape the mixture into 12 small patties, place on a plate, cover with plastic wrap, and refrigerate at least 2 hours or up to overnight.

Preheat the oven to 200°F. In a medium bowl, beat the eggs with the water. In another medium bowl, mix the flour with the remaining ½ teaspoon of salt and ¼ teaspoon of ground peppercorns. Dredge the cakes through the seasoned flour, tap off the excess, and then dip each of the cakes into the egg wash. End by dipping the cakes into the panko, pressing the panko into the cakes so it adheres. Place $\frac{1}{4}$ inch of canola oil in a large skillet and heat for 4 minutes over medium-high heat. Reduce the heat to medium and add one cake (if the oil immediately bubbles around the cake, then add a few more cakes and fry until golden brown, $1\frac{1}{2}$ to 2 minutes; if the oil doesn't bubble around the cake, continue to heat the oil for another 2 minutes before adding more cakes). Flip the cakes over and cook for $1\frac{1}{2}$ to 2 minutes to brown the other side. Transfer the cakes to a paper towel–lined baking sheet and place in the oven to stay warm. Fry the remaining cakes and serve hot or at room temperature with the aïoli.

CRAB AND SALMON CAKES are one of the most popular appetizers at my New York City restaurant, and the *New York Times* called them a perfect food to serve at Fourth of July parties. If you like, you can make the cakes larger to serve on a bun, like a burger. If doubling their size, fry for a few extra minutes so they brown properly. They pair excellently with a lager-style beer.

salads

In this chapter, I draw on the Indian sweet-sour-salty-spicy tradition, the premise behind many Indian foods, particularly salads. This tactic is especially important in chaats, the small snacks and saladlike dishes often served by street vendors or in simple restaurants. Say the word *chaat* to an Indian and he will begin to salivate in anticipation of the spicy, cool, and tangy flavors to come. Chaats often include the spice blend chaat masala, made from up to a dozen or so spices like dried mango peel powder (amchoor), dried pomegranate seed powder (anardana), toasted cumin, black salt, and ground ginger among others. Both the Sprouted Mung Bean Salad and the Crispy Okra Salad include chaat masala and are mainstays at my restaurant in New York City, where we serve the mung beans layered with crispy papadam and constructed into towers. **People love the fresh zing of the salad** and the crunch of the lentil wafers. If you can find papadam in your market or in an Indian grocery store, I encourage you to pair the two. The Crispy Okra Salad bursts with flavor from the chaat masala but also from the sharpness of red onions, the juiciness of tomatoes, and the fresh hit of lemon juice.

Even salads made without chaat masala can exhibit the same mouth-watering sweet-sour-salty-spicy characteristics. Fresh lemon juice and lots of scallions give the mellow asparagus in the Asparagus Salad a great tangy edge. The Corn Salad includes earthy cumin and fried ginger for some heat. It's incredibly easy to prepare with both in- or out-of-season corn, can be served hot or cold, and is good even a couple days later. Every region in India has its own version of kachoombar, an Indian chopped salad. While the principal ingredients, including tomatoes, cucumbers, onions, jalapeños, and cilantro, usually remain the same, the ratio of vegetables used and the degree of spiciness is up for interpretation. Fattoush, a Lebanese chopped salad, is such a treat when homemade. It's packed with vegetables, sumac-spiced crunchy pita chips, and fresh herbs like mint and cilantro. Both of these chopped salads are fantastic with grilled meats or kebabs.

Stir-Fried Carrot Salad is delicious as a salad, side dish, stuffing for enchiladas, or even wrapped into supermarket wonton wrappers and fried into homemade spring rolls. A little lime juice and lots of fresh herbs wake up classics like potato salad and fruit salad. My coauthor Raquel's toddler, Julian, loves munching on the mangoes in the Mango, Pineapple, and Grapefruit Salad while playing outside (she of course omits the chiles when making it for him), proving that it's never too early to develop a palate for mouth-tingling tastes.

slaw with mint, lime juice, chiles, and peanuts

SERVES 6 TO 8

A ¾-inch piece fresh ginger, peeled and grated

Juice of ½ lime

1½ teaspoons citrus vinegar or white wine vinegar

1½ tablespoons sugar

¾ teaspoon chaat masala

¼ teaspoon Toasted Cumin (page 16)

Pinch cayenne pepper

2 teaspoons kosher salt

¼ teaspoon ground peppercorns

9 scallions, thinly sliced

1 jalapeño (seeded and veined for less heat), finely chopped (optional)

1 pint cherry or grape tomatoes, halved

¼ cup finely chopped fresh cilantro

1 tablespoon finely chopped fresh mint leaves

½ head (1¼ pounds) green cabbage, halved, cored, and finely sliced

¼ cup chopped roasted peanuts

Whisk the ginger, lime juice, vinegar, sugar, chaat masala, toasted cumin, cayenne pepper, salt, and ground pepper together in a large bowl. Add the scallions, jalapeño, tomatoes, cilantro, and mint leaves and toss to combine. Add the cabbage and toss with your hands, making sure to coat it thoroughly with the other ingredients. The salad can be covered with plastic wrap and refrigerated for up to 4 hours at this point. Just before serving, sprinkle with the chopped peanuts.

MADE WITH absolutely no oil or mayonnaise, this tangy-spicy-crunchy-herby slaw will jolt your taste buds with its spice. It's fantastic served with stir-fried beef, chicken, or shrimp, or with grilled foods.

asparagus salad with lemon vinaigrette

SERVES 8

2 pounds thick-stalked asparagus, tough
    ends removed and stalks peeled

3 tablespoons canola oil or tea oil

2 tablespoons white wine, champagne, or
    citrus vinegar

1 lemon, zested and half juiced, the other
    half cut into wedges, for serving

¼ teaspoon kosher salt plus extra, for
    blanching

¼ teaspoon ground peppercorns

2 spring onions, or 8 scallions (white part
    only), thinly sliced on a diagonal

1 tomato, cored, halved, seeded, and
    thinly sliced

Place the asparagus in a baking dish and cover with water. Let it stand for 1 hour. While it soaks bring a large pot of salted water to a boil. Prepare an ice water bath and set it next to the sink.

Whisk the oil with the vinegar, lemon zest and juice, salt, and ground peppercorns in a large bowl. Add the onions and toss to coat in the vinaigrette.

Drain the asparagus and blanch in the boiling water for 3 to 5 minutes, or until it is al dente. Drain and transfer it to the ice water bath to cool. Drain again and transfer to your work surface. Thickly slice the asparagus on a diagonal and add it to the vinaigrette along with the tomato slices. Taste for seasoning and serve with the lemon wedges.

RENEE AND CARL, my dear friends from Seattle and also the owners and spirit behind the hugely successful Sur la Table stores, opened my eyes to the difference between thin and thick asparagus. Renee informed me that the fat spears are the cream of the crop, while the thin and delicate spears are really more akin to weeds. I also learned from her that soaking asparagus prior to cooking it plumps the stalks nicely, so they regain some of the moisture they lose after harvesting. I've eaten her asparagus and believe her completely on both counts. Though I usually don't bother to peel and soak asparagus, in this recipe it really does make a big difference. I like using tea oil (an oil made from cold pressing tea plants) in this salad. It's light, refined, and lovely with subtly flavored vegetables like asparagus, artichokes, and cardoons. If you don't have tea oil handy, substitute any neutral-flavored oil.

corn salad with peppers and ginger

SERVES 8

2 tablespoons canola oil or extra-virgin olive oil

1 teaspoon cumin seeds

3 dried red chiles (optional)

1 small red onion, finely chopped

2 medium red bell peppers, cored, seeded, and finely chopped

A 1½-inch piece fresh ginger, peeled and grated

½ jalapeño (cored and peeled if you prefer a milder flavor), finely chopped

2 teaspoons kosher salt

6 large ears of corn, husked, kernels sliced from the cob (about 5 cups of corn)

Heat the oil with the cumin and chiles (if using) in a large skillet or wok until the cumin is toasty, brown, and fragrant, about 2 minutes. Add the onion, cook for 1 minute, and then add the bell peppers, ginger, jalapeño, and salt and cook until the onion has softened, 2 to 3 more minutes. Add the corn and cook until it's tender, 2 to 4 minutes. Transfer the salad to a bowl and serve hot, at room temperature, or chilled.

EVERY YEAR my good friend Art Smith, an incredibly talented chef, invites some of his colleagues to join him in helping to raise money for various charitable causes. For one of these events I decided to make Corn Salad, and it became the talk of the evening, with guests lining up for second and third helpings. It's the kind of dish that is deceptively easy, tasting so good that no one will ever believe it took you less than 15 minutes to make. It's especially delicious in late summer when field corn is at its peak and is so milky and sweet that you barely need to cook it.

avocado salad

SERVES 8

2 tablespoons extra-virgin olive oil
Juice of 1 lime
$\frac{1}{2}$ teaspoon Toasted Cumin (page 16)
$\frac{1}{2}$ teaspoon kosher salt
$\frac{1}{2}$ recipe Ginger-Pickled Onions (page 17)
4 cups arugula, washed and tough stems removed

3 large tomatoes, cored and cut into chunks
$\frac{1}{2}$ cup roughly chopped fresh cilantro leaves
$\frac{1}{2}$ jalapeño (cored and seeded if you prefer a milder flavor), finely chopped
4 avocados, halved, pitted, peeled, and cut into large chunks

Whisk the oil, lime juice, Toasted Cumin, and salt together in a large bowl. Add the Pickled Onions, arugula, tomatoes, cilantro, and jalapeño and toss to combine. Add the avocados and gently toss with the other ingredients so they don't break down. Taste for seasoning and serve.

THOUGH THE INGREDIENTS in this salad are similar to guacamole, the taste of these two dishes couldn't be more different. Cutting the avocado in large chunks highlights its buttery texture and sublime smoothness.

creamy potato salad

SERVES 8 TO 10

4 large eggs
¾ cup mayonnaise
2 tablespoons canola oil
2 tablespoons champagne or white wine
  vinegar
Juice of 1 lime
1½ tablespoons Dijon mustard
3 tablespoons sugar
1 tablespoon plus 1 teaspoon kosher salt
½ teaspoon ground peppercorns

⅛ teaspoon cayenne pepper
2 bunches of scallions (white and light
  green part only), thinly sliced
¼ cup chopped sweet gherkins
1 generous cup finely chopped fresh
  basil or dill
¼ cup fresh parsley, finely chopped
3½ pounds red potatoes (about 8 small to
  medium), peeled, halved and each half
  quartered

Place the eggs in a medium saucepan and cover with water. Cover, bring to a boil, and turn off the heat. Let the eggs stand 10 minutes in the hot water and then drain and cool. Once cool, peel and separate the whites from the yolks. Quarter the whites and set aside. Finely mash the yolks.

Whisk the mayonnaise, egg yolks, oil, vinegar, lime juice, mustard, sugar, 1 teaspoon salt, ground peppercorns, and cayenne pepper together in a large bowl. Stir in the scallions, gherkins, basil or dill, and parsley. Cover with plastic wrap and refrigerate.

Place the potatoes in a large pot and cover with 1 inch of water. Bring the potatoes to a boil, add 1 tablespoon of kosher salt, reduce heat to a medium simmer, and cook until the potatoes are just tender, 15 to 20 minutes. Drain the potatoes, and while still warm, add them to the dressing and toss to combine. Press plastic wrap onto the surface of the salad and refrigerate until thoroughly chilled, at least 2 hours or up to 1 day in advance. Taste for seasoning, and then gently fold in the quartered egg whites and serve.

ED SCHOENFELD, a restaurant consultant and chef, makes a version of this potato salad for many of his dinner parties. Before I met Ed, I was never a fan of mayonnaise-based potato salad. Once I tasted his version, however, my opinion changed forever. What's unusual about this dish is that there is a touch of sugar in it. The sweetness combines with the sweet-sour taste of the gherkins, the tang of the lime, the spiciness of the cayenne, and the herby freshness of the basil to make a potato salad that hits the ground running. Since it contains lots of mayonnaise and olive oil, I admit that it isn't the healthiest salad in this chapter, but since it's not the kind of salad that you make every day, it's worth the splurge.

sprouted mung bean salad

SERVES 8

3 cups sprouted mung beans
1 small red onion, finely chopped
1 large or 2 small ripe tomatoes, cored
  and finely chopped
1 small cucumber, peeled, seeded, and
  finely chopped
1 jalapeño (cored and seeded if you prefer
  a milder flavor), finely minced

½ cup chopped fresh cilantro leaves
½ teaspoon Toasted Cumin (page 16)
½ teaspoon chaat masala (optional)
1 teaspoon kosher salt
¼ teaspoon cayenne pepper (optional)
Juice of 1 lime

Place the mung beans, onion, tomato, cucumber, jalapeño, and cilantro in a large bowl and toss together. Add the Toasted Cumin and chaat masala, salt, cayenne pepper (if using), and lime juice and mix well. Chill for at least 1 hour or up to 4 hours. Taste for seasoning and serve.

THIS IS A COMMON street food that can be found all over northern India. In southern and western India, it's commonly made with fresh grated coconut and even more chiles. It's a signature dish on my New York City restaurant's menu. Serve it solo or with lentil wafers (papadum).

indian chopped mixed salad

(kachoombar salad)

SERVES 8

2 large tomatoes, chopped

1 large cucumber (preferably an English cucumber), seeded and finely chopped

1 medium red onion, finely chopped

1 jalapeño pepper (cored and seeded if you prefer a milder flavor), finely diced

½ cup chopped fresh cilantro leaves

1 teaspoon Toasted Cumin (page 16)

1½ teaspoons kosher salt

¼ teaspoon cayenne pepper

¼ teaspoon ground peppercorns

Juice of 1 lime

Toss all of the ingredients together in a large bowl. Taste for seasoning, adding more salt, lime juice, or cayenne pepper if necessary, and serve.

THIS IS THE INDIAN VERSION of Fattoush (page 61) but without the bread and the oil. I grew up eating this salad in New Delhi, especially during the sweltering summer months. In the summer when fruits were at their peak, Mom would add any combination of sliced bananas, chopped apples, seedless grapes, chopped guava, chopped pineapple, and orange segments to the salad along with a half teaspoon of chaat masala for a delicious sweet-and-sour salad. I generally peel my cucumbers, but if yours is unwaxed, you may leave it unpeeled if you prefer.

stir-fried carrot salad

SERVES 8

2 tablespoons canola oil or extra-virgin olive oil

1 jalapeño (cored and seeded if you prefer a milder flavor), finely chopped

1 teaspoon cumin seeds

½ teaspoon ground peppercorns

1 teaspoon ground coriander

10 medium carrots (about 1 pound), peeled and grated

1 head green cabbage, cored and shredded

½ cup chopped fresh cilantro

½ teaspoon cayenne pepper

2 teaspoons sugar

1 teaspoon Toasted Cumin (page 16)

1 tablespoon kosher salt

Juice of 1½ limes

Heat the oil with the jalapeño, cumin seeds, and ground peppercorns in a large skillet or wok over medium-high heat, cooking until the cumin is fragrant and browned, about 2 minutes. Add the coriander, cook for 15 seconds, and then add the carrots and cabbage. Cook, stirring occasionally, until the cabbage has wilted yet is still al dente, about 4 minutes.

Stir in the cilantro, cayenne pepper, sugar, Toasted Cumin, and salt. Cook for 30 seconds and then remove the skillet from the heat. Stir in the lime juice and taste for seasoning. Serve either warm, at room temperature, or cold.

A CARROT SALAD is bright and festive, great for picnics and barbecues. The carrots bleed their orange color into the cabbage, making it a warm orange-yellow, like the color of turmeric. The carrots are cooked just enough to eliminate their raw sharpness; the cabbage remains al dente, with a nice, toothsome snap. Grate the carrots and cabbage by hand or using the slicer attachment on your food processor or stand mixer. Note that using a machine will result in a finer texture.

fattoush

SERVES 8

½ cup extra-virgin olive oil plus extra, for greasing the foil

1 large cucumber, peeled, seeded, and finely chopped

1 teaspoon kosher salt

2 pieces pita bread, chopped or torn into bite-sized pieces

Juice of 2 lemons plus 1 lemon cut into wedges, for serving

1 teaspoon ground sumac (optional)

2 garlic cloves, peeled and finely minced

½ teaspoon ground peppercorns

½ head romaine lettuce, chopped or roughly torn

8 radishes, washed, trimmed, and finely chopped

3 medium tomatoes, cored and finely chopped

3 scallions (white and green parts), thinly sliced

½ cup chopped fresh cilantro leaves

¼ cup chopped fresh mint leaves

¼ cup chopped fresh parsley leaves

Preheat the oven to 400°F. Line a baking sheet with aluminum foil, grease the foil with a little oil, and set it aside. Place the cucumber in a colander, toss with ½ teaspoon of the salt, and set it aside for 30 minutes over a plate to drain.

Toss the pita bread with a quarter of the lemon juice and the sumac (if using) in a large bowl and let it sit for 5 minutes. Arrange the seasoned pita in an even layer on the prepared baking sheet and bake until crispy and dry, 12 to 15 minutes, turning the pita chips over after 7 minutes. (You can toast the pita on a wire rack set over a baking sheet; place them diagonally across the rack so they don't fall through the openings. Since the air circulates beneath and above the pita, you don't have to turn it midway through; note that the pita will probably take less time to toast.)

Whisk the remaining lemon juice with the oil, garlic, ½ teaspoon salt, and ground peppercorns in a large bowl. Add the cucumbers, lettuce, radishes, tomatoes, scallions, cilantro, mint, and parsley and toss to combine. Add the pita, toss to incorporate, taste for seasoning, and serve immediately with the lemon wedges.

NAJWA SARKIS STONE, a proud Lebanese American, makes some of the most delicious and addictive Middle Eastern food. She is a hostess with great style and élan, and an invitation to her home is like a call to a presidential gala. Tart, crispy, crunchy, and herbal, Najwa's rendition of fattoush is the best I've tried after eating this dish around the country and the world. Don't panic if you can't find the sumac. Many Lebanese cooks omit it and you can, too.

mango, pineapple, and grapefruit salad with chile-lime vinaigrette

SERVES 6 TO 8

FOR THE SALAD

2 pink grapefruits, peeled, pith sliced off, fruit divided into segments, and segments cut in half

4 semiripe mangoes, peeled and chopped

1 ripe pineapple, peeled, cored, and chopped

3 tablespoons sugar

FOR THE VINAIGRETTE

2 tablespoons canola oil or tea oil

2 tablespoons white wine, champagne, or citrus vinegar

1/2 jalapeño (cored and seeded if you prefer a milder flavor), finely chopped

1/2 cup chopped fresh mint leaves

1/2 cup chopped fresh cilantro leaves

1/2 lime, zested and juiced

1 tablespoon sugar

Pinch of cayenne pepper

1/2 teaspoon kosher salt

1/2 teaspoon ground peppercorns

To make the salad, toss the grapefruit with the mangoes, pineapple, and sugar in a large bowl. Cover with plastic wrap and refrigerate for 1 hour.

To make the vinaigrette, whisk together the vinaigrette ingredients in a medium bowl. Pour over the fruit, toss to combine, and serve.

WHEN TESTING THIS RECIPE, I was lucky to have my mother visiting from India. I asked her to try a bite, and it actually made her blush! For Mom to have reacted this way, and to a salad no less, made me realize that the recipe had been perfected. To save time, I buy precut pineapple at the grocery store. It makes taking the extra minute required to segment the grapefruit seem like less of a chore. This salad is superb with grilled fish or chicken, but it also makes a light and refreshingly different dessert.

crispy okra salad (kararee bhindi)

SERVES 4

Canola oil

1 pound okra, stemmed and thinly sliced
   lengthwise

½ small red onion, thinly sliced

1 medium or 2 small tomatoes, cored,
   seeded, and thinly sliced

¼ cup chopped fresh cilantro leaves

Juice of ½ lemon

1 teaspoon kosher salt

1½ teaspoons chaat masala

Heat 2 inches of oil in a large heavy-bottomed pot to 350°F. Add a third of the okra and fry until browned and crisp, 5 to 7 minutes. Transfer to a paper towel–lined plate and repeat with the remaining okra, making sure the oil temperature comes back to 350°F before frying additional batches.

In a large bowl, toss the okra with the onion, tomato, cilantro, lemon juice, salt, and chaat masala. Taste for seasoning and serve immediately.

THIS ISN'T A TRADITIONAL RECIPE, but something Panditji, my family's Brahman chef, and I came up with when I was ten years old. Originally we slit the okra in half lengthwise and marinated them with chickpea flour, lemon juice, and spices. Since coming to the United States, I have streamlined the recipe and now I find it more addictive than ever. Many of my friends proclaim it to be the ideal substitute for French fries. Although I think of this as a salad, others call it a side dish. You decide.

soups and stews

I came to America in 1993 with big dreams and aspirations, and I shared many of these with Mary Ann Joulwan, one of my first, and still one of my closest, friends. My first winter in New York City was a cold one, rife with snowstorms and subzero temperatures. I recall trudging through frigid Central Park, over snowbanks and up icy sidewalks to Mary Ann's apartment, not in a pair of snow boots or even sneakers but instead wearing my flimsy leather flip-flops, more appropriate for July in New Delhi than January in New York City!

Though Mary Ann eyed my less-than-appropriate footwear with skepticism, like my parents she never judged or scolded. Instead, she greeted me unconditionally with a steamy bowl of homemade soup. Within minutes we'd be sitting side by side on her sofa eating soup (most often my favorite lentil soup), watching *Jeopardy,* and catching up on each other's adventures.

I was thousands of miles from India, but **a simple bowl of soup made me feel at home**. There is a Hindu saying, *atithi deva bhaav,* which means that when guests enter your house, God comes with them. The ultimate way to honor houseguests in southern India is to greet them with rasam, a fragrantly spiced Indian consommé. I was comforted to discover that though the soup was different, the custom transcended continents and cultures.

My soups and stews are Indian in spirit with an American approach, meaning that they are flavorful and vibrant yet simple to prepare. When it comes to preparing soups and stews, a stocked arsenal of readily available spices and aromatics is key to cutting other time-consuming steps, like making stocks and broths. Oil and spice infusions that take just minutes to make yield deep flavors and memorable results. My mom taught me that **the best way to thicken soups naturally is with a few tablespoons of lentils, split peas, or mashed legumes.** They contribute a pleasant texture and added nutrition. When I need to convert a chunky soup to something more elegant, I reach for my handheld immersion blender. It does the job in seconds, creating a creamy soup as appropriate in a china tureen as it is in an insulated travel mug, and also saves me from dirtying my blender. Most of these soups and stews can be frozen and eaten at a later date, which comes in handy, especially when you feel a bit lazy yet still crave something homemade.

Often crafted from staples that can be found in your refrigerator and pantry, soups and stews have the magical ability to nourish and heal, sate and celebrate all that is at once wondrous and easy about food.

creamy vegetable soup

SERVES 8

¼ cup canola oil or extra-virgin olive oil
¼ cup yellow split peas (channa dal)
1 dried red chile
½ teaspoon Garam Masala (page 20)
2 teaspoons ground peppercorns
8 ounces asparagus, tough ends removed
 and chopped
1 medium potato, peeled and quartered
1 medium onion (red, white, or yellow),
 quartered
1 medium tomato, quartered

½ head cauliflower, cut into florets
10 ounces button mushrooms, rinsed or
 brushed clean and halved if large
2 large red bell peppers, cored, seeded,
 and chopped
3 Parmigiano-Reggiano rinds (optional)
 plus some grated cheese, for serving
1½ tablespoons kosher salt
8 cups water
⅓ cup heavy cream, half-and-half, or
 skim or whole milk

Heat the oil with the split peas, chile, Garam Masala, and ground peppercorns in a large pot over medium-high heat until the chile is dark, stirring occasionally, for about 3 minutes. Add the vegetables, the cheese rinds, and the salt and cook for 3 minutes. Add the water and cream and bring to a boil. Reduce the heat to a gentle simmer and cook until the potatoes and cauliflower easily mash against the side of the pot, about 20 minutes.

Transfer some of the soup to a blender (don't fill blender more than two-thirds full), cover, and pulse to release some heat. Blend the soup until it is smooth and pour into a clean pot. Repeat with the remaining soup.

Bring the soup back to a boil. Reduce the heat to medium-low and simmer until it thickens slightly, 5 to 6 minutes. Taste for seasoning and serve sprinkled with grated cheese.

IN INDIA, spices, legumes, nuts, and grains are employed both as flavor agents and thickeners. They're also a great way to add protein to your diet, and with veggies and other starches, they create a complex protein that is healthy for the body. I often make this soup at the end of the week when I need to clean out my refrigerator. In addition to the vegetables listed alone, feel free to add butternut squash, cabbage, carrots, kale, leeks, mustard greens, peas, scallions, spinach, zucchini, and one green bell pepper (it provides a nice bitterness). I find about 14 cups of chopped vegetables to be a good benchmark for a lovely, creamy soup. Use an immersion blender to puree the soup right in the pot.

creamy cauliflower and spinach soup

SERVES 10 TO 12

4 tablespoons (½ stick) unsalted butter

2 tablespoons canola oil or extra-virgin olive oil

1 tablespoon finely chopped fresh rosemary

1 tablespoon finely chopped fresh thyme

1 teaspoon ground peppercorns

1 medium red onion, chopped

4 garlic cloves, peeled

1 large or 2 small heads cauliflower, cut into florets (about 3½ pounds)

1 small red potato, peeled and chopped

1 pound spinach, washed and tough stems removed

1 cup milk

2 tablespoons kosher salt

8 cups water

Place the butter, oil, rosemary, thyme, and ground peppercorns in a large pot and heat over medium-high until the butter is melted and the rosemary is fragrant, about 2 minutes. Add the onion and garlic and cook until they are soft, stirring often, about 3 minutes. Add the cauliflower and potato and cook for 3 minutes. Add the spinach, milk, salt, and water and bring to a boil. Reduce the heat to a gentle simmer, cover, and cook until the cauliflower easily mashes against the side of the pot, about 30 minutes.

Transfer some of the soup to a blender (don't fill blender more than two-thirds full), cover, and pulse to release some heat. Blend the soup until it is completely smooth and pour into a clean pot. Repeat with the remaining soup. Bring the soup back to a boil, taste for seasoning, and serve.

CREAMY, rich, and flavorful, it's hard to believe that this soup is virtually fat free and takes less than an hour to make from start to finish. It is a great example of a comforting and nutritious soup that can be served as a quick meal on its own, or as the first course to a more elaborate dinner. It can be served as is or with small bits of butter-fried cauliflower sprinkled on top.

spring vegetable vichyssoise

SERVES 8

FOR THE VICHYSSOISE
2 tablespoons unsalted butter
2 tablespoons canola oil
1 teaspoon ground peppercorns
¼ teaspoon freshly grated nutmeg
¼ head (about ¾ pound) cabbage, cored
  and chopped
2 zucchini, thickly sliced
12 scallions (white and light green parts
  only), thinly sliced
4 large leeks (white parts only), cleaned
  and chopped

1 large red potato, peeled and chopped
2 tablespoons kosher salt
2 teaspoons sugar
1 cup milk
5 cups water
Chopped chives, for serving

FOR THE CROUTONS
½ baguette, thinly sliced
4 tablespoons (½ stick) unsalted butter,
  melted

To make the vichyssoise, place the butter, oil, ground peppercorns, and ⅛ teaspoon of the nutmeg in a large pot and heat over medium-high until the butter melts, about 1 minute. Add the vegetables, salt, and sugar and cook until they are just starting to brown, about 4 minutes, stirring occasionally. Pour in the milk and 5 cups of water and bring to a boil. Reduce the heat to medium-low, cover, and simmer until the potatoes easily mash against the side of the pot, 25 to 30 minutes. Turn off the heat and let the soup stand for 20 minutes.

Preheat the oven to 450°F. To make the croutons, brush both sides of the baguette slices with melted butter and place them on a baking sheet. Toast until browned and crisp, 3 to 4 minutes, and then set aside.

Transfer a third of the soup to a blender (don't fill more than two-thirds full) and pulse to release some heat. Blend until the soup is completely smooth. Pour the soup into a clean pot and repeat with the remaining soup. Add the remaining ⅛ teaspoon of nutmeg and bring the soup to a simmer. Taste for seasoning and serve sprinkled with chopped chives and topped with a toasted baguette slice.

BACK IN MY CATERING DAYS, I was hired to cook for the Young Presidents' Organization, a group of business leaders under the age of forty. The president of the club asked me to make vichyssoise with an Indian bent for one of their gatherings. Instead of using the classic potato-leek-cream trilogy, I added multiple spring vegetables and used milk instead of cream. The soup was—and still is—a huge success whether served warm in the winter (the miracle of America—year-round spring vegetables!) or chilled in the summertime.

spicy indian shrimp consommé (rasam)

FOR THE SHRIMP

2 pounds shell-on medium shrimp,
    shelled and deveined (reserve the shells
    for broth)
1 teaspoon kosher salt
1 teaspoon ground coriander
½ teaspoon cracked peppercorns
¼ teaspoon cayenne pepper

FOR THE BROTH

Reserved shrimp shells
1 red onion, chopped
12 curry leaves (optional)
11 whole black peppercorns
6 whole cloves
2 dried red chiles
A ½-inch piece cinnamon stick
8 cups water

2 medium tomatoes, cored and diced
1 cup canned chopped tomatoes
1 tablespoon kosher salt
1 teaspoon Sambhaar (page 21),
    or ½ teaspoon curry powder
1 teaspoon ground coriander
½ teaspoon ground peppercorns
¼ teaspoon cayenne pepper

FOR THE TEMPERING OIL

3 tablespoons canola oil
24 curry leaves (optional)
2 dried red chiles (optional)
2 teaspoons mustard seeds
1 teaspoon ground cumin
¼ cup unsweetened shredded coconut
Juice of 1 lemon

Combine the shrimp, salt, coriander, ground peppercorns, and cayenne pepper in a gallon-sized resealable plastic bag, and refrigerate while you make the broth.

Bring the reserved shrimp shells, onions, curry leaves (if using), peppercorns, cloves, chiles, cinnamon stick, and water to a boil in a large pot. Reduce the heat to medium-low, cover, and simmer for 30 minutes. Strain the broth through a mesh sieve and into another large pot, pressing on the shrimp shells to extract as much liquid from them as possible. Add the remaining broth ingredients. Bring to a boil, reduce the heat to medium-low, and simmer for 10 minutes.

Make the tempering oil. Heat the oil with the curry leaves (if using), chiles (if using), mustard seeds, and cumin in a medium skillet over medium-high heat until the spices are fragrant, about 1 minute. Add the coconut and fry while stirring until light golden, 30 seconds to 1 minute. Scrape the spices and coconut into the broth. Add the shrimp and poach in the simmering broth until curled and opaque, 1 to 2 minutes. Add the lemon juice, taste for seasoning, and serve.

A STUDENT in one of my cooking classes recently dubbed this soup a "tomato cappuccino," because "the spices wake you up instantly." Though this consommé seems quite fancy, at its heart it is nothing more than a pantry soup, with shrimp from your freezer and spices from your pantry. You can make it in under one hour.

mary ann's french lentil soup with cilantro and orzo

SERVES 8

13 cups water
6 tablespoons extra-virgin olive oil
2 teaspoons cumin seeds
3 dried red chiles
¼ teaspoon ground peppercorns
1 large red onion, quartered and sliced
  crosswise

2 tablespoons kosher salt
2 cups green French lentils
½ teaspoon turmeric
¼ cup orzo pasta
Chopped fresh cilantro, for serving
Lemon wedges, for serving

Place 1 cup of water next to your stovetop. Heat the oil with the cumin in a large heavy-bottomed pot over medium-high heat until the cumin is browned, about 2 minutes. Add the chiles and ground peppercorns and cook for 30 seconds. Add the onion and the salt and cook until the onion is deep browned and crispy, 15 to 20 minutes. Stir often and splash the pot with water (you may not need the full cup), scraping browned bits from the bottom of the pot when the onions begin to stick. Add 2 cups of water along with the lentils and the turmeric to the pot and cook for 5 minutes, stirring occasionally. Add 10 more cups of water and bring to a boil. Reduce the heat to a gentle simmer, cover, and cook for 20 minutes, stirring midway through.

Stir in the orzo and return the soup to a boil. Cook, partially covered, until the orzo is al dente, about 10 minutes. Cover the pot and turn off the heat. Let the soup stand for 30 minutes to 2 hours to thicken. Before serving, bring to a boil, reduce the heat to medium-low, and simmer for 10 minutes. Taste for seasoning and serve sprinkled with cilantro and with a lemon wedge.

I LEARNED TO MAKE this hearty and comforting soup from my good friend Mary Ann Joulwan. A version appeared in my first cookbook, *Indian Home Cooking*; I've since simplified the recipe, making it from start to finish in one pot. Deeply browning the onions until they're very dark and crisp is the secret to the soup's amazing, deep flavor. I splash the onions with water every few minutes to prevent them from sticking and burning. The water creates steam that unglues the onions and cools the pot ever so slightly, letting me take the onions to an even browner state. I use this technique in many recipes throughout the book, like in Smoky Bean Soup (page 77) and Imm Jaddara (page 96). This soup really reaches its peak of flavor 2 to 3 days after it is made.

smoky bean soup

SERVES 8

6 cups water
¼ cup extra-virgin olive oil
10 whole black peppercorns
8 whole cloves
4 dried bay leaves
4 dried red chiles
A 1-inch piece cinnamon stick
2 large red onions, chopped
2 tablespoons kosher salt
½ pound thick-cut bacon, finely chopped

2 medium parsnips, peeled and sliced into rounds
5 garlic cloves, peeled and roughly chopped
2 cups dried cannellini beans soaked in cool water overnight and drained (if using canned beans, see below)
12 scallions (white and light green part only), thinly sliced
Pinch of asafetida (optional)
Lemon wedges, for serving

Place 1 cup of water next to your stovetop. Heat the oil with the black peppercorns, cloves, bay leaves, chiles, and cinnamon in a large pot over medium-high heat until the cinnamon unfurls, 2 to 3 minutes. Add the onions and salt and cook until the onions are soft and browned, 6 to 8 minutes, stirring occasionally. Stir in the bacon, parsnips, and garlic and cook until the onions are deeply brown, about 10 minutes longer. Stir often, splashing the pot with water (you may not need the full cup) and scraping browned bits from the bottom of the pot if the onions or bacon begin to stick. Add the cannellini beans, scallions, and asafetida (if using) and cook for 2 minutes. Pour in 5 cups of water and bring to a boil. Reduce the heat to a gentle simmer, cover, and cook until the beans are tender, 1½ to 2 hours, stirring every 20 minutes. Taste for seasoning and serve with a lemon wedge.

THIS BEAN SOUP is hearty, smoky, and rich. Instead of using a chicken or vegetable stock, I build flavor by frying the spices in oil before adding the vegetables, bacon, and beans. When used together, spices like red chiles, bay, cloves, cinnamon, and peppercorns make what I like to think of as the Indian version of a bouquet garni. For a faster soup, use 4½ cups canned and rinsed cannellini beans (or other white beans), add them with the scallions, and cook for 30 minutes instead of 1½ to 2 hours. In India, we often add a pinch of asafetida to dishes with beans. Not only does it lend an elusive, garlic-onion flavor, but it also aids in digesting the beans.

lentil and vegetable stew (dhansaak)

SERVES 8 TO 10

FOR THE SPICE BLEND
A 1-inch piece cinnamon stick
6 green cardamom pods
1 tablespoon coriander seeds
2 teaspoons cumin seeds
1 teaspoon fennel seeds
1 teaspoon mustard seeds
1 teaspoon turmeric
½ teaspoon whole black peppercorns
¼ teaspoon fenugreek seeds
¼ teaspoon whole cloves

FOR THE HERB PASTE
½ cup loosely packed fresh cilantro
½ cup loosely packed fresh mint leaves
A 3-inch piece fresh ginger, peeled and
  roughly chopped
1 jalapeño (cored and seeded if you prefer
  a milder flavor), roughly chopped
3 dried red chiles

5 garlic cloves, peeled and roughly
  chopped
¼ cup water

FOR THE STEW
9 cups water
¼ cup plus 3 tablespoons canola oil or
  extra-virgin olive oil
1 teaspoon cumin seeds
2 red onions, finely diced, plus 1 red
  onion, chopped
1 tablespoon plus 2 teaspoons kosher salt
2½ cups lentils (a combination of brown,
  green, red, and yellow lentils)
2 large tomatoes, chopped
1¼-pound eggplant, cut into 1-inch
  chunks
1½ cups frozen corn, or fresh corn
  kernels (from 2 ears)

To make the spice blend, grind all the ingredients in a coffee grinder or small food processor until powder fine and set aside.

To make the herb paste, blend all the ingredients in a food processor until smooth and set aside.

To make the stew, place 1 cup of water next to your stovetop. Heat ¼ cup oil and the cumin seeds in a large pot over medium-high heat until the cumin is toasted and browned, about 2 minutes. Add the finely diced onions and the salt and cook until the onions are deep brown, 12 to 15 minutes. Stir often and splash with water, scraping up any browned bits from the bottom of the pot when the onions begin to stick. Add whatever water remains from the cup and cook until it evaporates, about 3 minutes.

Reduce the heat to medium, add the lentils and 3 tablespoons of the spice blend, and cook for 2 minutes, stirring often. Add an additional 8 cups of water, bring to a boil, reduce the heat to medium-low, cover, and simmer for 30 minutes, stirring often.

Meanwhile, heat the remaining 3 tablespoons of olive oil in a medium skillet over medium-high heat for 30 seconds. Add the herb paste and cook it for 2 minutes while stirring. Once the lentils have cooked 30 minutes, add the cooked herb paste and the tomatoes, eggplant, corn, and chopped onion to the pot. Bring everything to a boil and add the remaining spice blend. Reduce the heat to medium-low, cover, and cook until the eggplant is completely soft, about 45 minutes, stirring every 10 minutes. Taste for seasoning and serve.

VARIATION: Autumn Vegetable Dhansaak

Once the onions are deep brown, add $\frac{1}{4}$ pound chopped turnips, $\frac{1}{4}$ pound halved radishes, and $1\frac{1}{4}$ pounds chopped sweet potatoes, sugar pumpkin, or yams. Cook 3 minutes, reduce the heat to medium, add the lentils, and proceed with the recipe as instructed, eliminating the tomatoes, eggplant, and corn from the recipe.

THIS IS A PARSI STEW. Many of the ancestors of today's Parsi Zoroastrian community arrived in Gujarat, a state on the west coast of India, by boat in the tenth century. They asked the king for asylum from religious persecution in Persia. As a response, the king sent them a glass brimming with milk to symbolize that the country was already as full of people as the glass was full of milk. The Parsi leader added sugar to a glass of milk and sent it back to the king, saying that like the sugar in the milk, his community would sweeten the daily lives of the region but never be a visible nuisance. This has become the reality of the Parsi people. Centuries later, they have not only sweetened the Indian diaspora with their generosity of spirit, but their philanthropic establishments have enriched the lives of millions.

In this stew each type of lentil adds its own unique attributes: whole brown masoor dal is used for texture, fiber, and its creamy consistency; yellow split peas, also called channa dal, are used for their high protein content and rich, nutty aroma; salmon pink washed masoor dal is used for creamy quality that comes without much fiber. Though this stew is delicious served the same day it is made, it becomes even more beautiful the longer it is allowed to sit. I like to make it a couple days ahead.

moroccan-style lamb stew

SERVES 8

FOR THE LAMB

2 pounds cubed lamb stew meat
(preferably from the shoulder)
1 teaspoon ground cumin
½ teaspoon paprika
½ teaspoon turmeric
1 tablespoon kosher salt
1 teaspoon ground peppercorns
Juice of ½ lime plus 1 lime cut into
wedges, for serving

FOR THE STEW

¼ cup canola oil or extra-virgin olive oil
2 tablespoons unsalted butter
6 green cardamom pods
A 2-inch piece cinnamon stick
¼ teaspoon whole cloves
¼ teaspoon red pepper flakes
¼ teaspoon whole black peppercorns
A 1½-inch piece fresh ginger, peeled and
minced

2 (15-ounce) cans chickpeas, drained and
rinsed
1½ pounds turnips, peeled and chopped
into thick cubes
2 red onions, halved, and each half cut in
thirds lengthwise
2 medium carrots, peeled and thickly
sliced
1 large red potato, peeled, halved
lengthwise and thickly sliced
2 garlic cloves, peeled and smashed
1 teaspoon ground coriander
¼ teaspoon cayenne pepper (optional)
¼ teaspoon ground ginger
¼ teaspoon mace
1 tablespoon kosher salt
2 cups chopped tomatoes
2½ cups water
½ cup chopped fresh cilantro
Lime wedges, for serving

To prepare the lamb, place the lamb, the cumin, paprika, turmeric, salt, ground peppercorns, and lime juice in a large bowl, and toss to coat. Cover, and refrigerate for 30 minutes, or up to 3 hours.

To make the stew, place the oil, butter, cardamom, cinnamon stick, cloves, pepper flakes, and whole peppercorns in a large pot over medium-high heat until the butter melts, 1 to 2 minutes. Add the ginger and cook until it is just starting to brown, about 1½ minutes, stirring often. Add the lamb (discard any remaining marinade) and stir to coat with the spices. Cook until the lamb just begins to brown, 3 to 5 minutes.

Mash ½ cup of the chickpeas and set aside. Stir in the remaining whole chickpeas, turnips, onions, carrots, potato, and garlic into the lamb and cook for 10 minutes, stirring often. Add the ground coriander, cayenne pepper (if using), ground ginger, mace, and salt. Cook until the pot is nearly dry, about 5 minutes.

Add the tomatoes, mashed chickpeas, and water and bring to a boil. Reduce the heat to medium-low, cover, and simmer until the lamb is fall-apart tender and the turnips easily break apart, 2 to 2$\frac{1}{2}$ hours, stirring every 20 minutes. Sprinkle with cilantro and taste for seasoning. Serve with lime wedges.

LAMB STEW is a favorite dinner to many Indian Muslims. A visit to Morocco inspired this version, with nuances of flavors that I experienced there, like paprika and chickpeas. Adding mashed chickpeas to soup is a time-tested Indian technique that lends texture and depth. Along with the tomatoes, the mashed chickpeas act as a thickening agent, giving the stew nice body. This is a good slow cooker recipe—after browning the meat and vegetables, transfer them along with the remaining spices and liquids to your slow cooker and serve over couscous or rice.

chicken-chickpea harira

SERVES 8

⅓ cup extra-virgin olive oil

1 teaspoon ground peppercorns

5 whole cloves

A 1-inch piece cinnamon stick

2 red onions, finely diced

1½ pounds boneless chicken thigh meat, cut into small cubes

½ teaspoon turmeric

1 teaspoon Aleppo pepper, or ¼ teaspoon cayenne pepper

1 tablespoon plus 1 teaspoon kosher salt

3 medium tomatoes, cored and diced

2 (15-ounce) cans chickpeas, drained and rinsed

2 cups canned chopped tomatoes

3 cups water

½ teaspoon saffron threads, finely ground

1 teaspoon Toasted Cumin (page 16)

½ teaspoon Garam Masala (page 20), Sambhaar (page 21), or curry powder

¼ cup chopped fresh cilantro

Heat the oil with the ground peppercorns, cloves, and cinnamon stick in a large pot over medium-high heat for 1 minute. Add the onions and cook until they're soft and lightly browned around the edges, 3 to 5 minutes, stirring often. Add the chicken and cook until the meat releases its liquid and the pan dries, about 5 minutes, stirring occasionally.

Mix in the turmeric, Aleppo pepper, and salt and cook for 4 minutes, stirring occasionally. Add the fresh tomatoes and cook until they release their juices, about 3½ minutes, stirring often and scraping any browned bits from the bottom of the pot. Add the chickpeas, canned tomatoes, and water and bring to a boil. Reduce the heat to medium-low, cover, and simmer for 35 minutes. Stir in the saffron, Toasted Cumin, Garam Masala, and the chopped cilantro. Taste for seasoning and serve.

HARIRA IS A MOROCCAN SOUP that is served during Ramadan to break the day's fast. It is most often prepared with lamb and perfumed with spices like turmeric and cinnamon. Boneless chicken thigh meat generally has a silkier texture and more depth of flavor than chicken breast meat (though chicken breast meat can be easily substituted if you prefer). My favorite saffron comes from Kashmir, a state in northern India. Its color, aroma, and taste are headier than Spanish or Persian saffron, and its depth of flavor and color is stronger. To get the most flavor from saffron, use a mortar and pestle to grind the threads into a fine powder.

spiced beef and vegetable stew

SERVES 8

1½ pounds cubed beef stew meat
  (preferably beef chuck)
2 tablespoons plus 1 teaspoon salt
1 teaspoon ground peppercorns
¼ cup extra-virgin olive oil
3 tablespoons unsalted butter
3 dried red chiles (optional)
A 1-inch piece cinnamon stick
¼ teaspoon cumin seeds
¼ teaspoon loosely packed saffron threads
2 medium red onions, halved and each
  half quartered

2 medium red potatoes, peeled, halved
  and each half quartered
6 ounces radishes (about 20 small), ends
  trimmed
2 garlic cloves, peeled and smashed
3 medium carrots, peeled and grated
1½ teaspoons ground cumin
1½ teaspoons ground coriander
½ teaspoon sweet paprika
2 cups ripe fresh or canned chopped
  tomatoes
2 cups water

Place the beef in a large bowl and toss with 1 teaspoon kosher salt and the ground pepper-corns. Cover with plastic wrap and refrigerate for 30 minutes, or up to 3 hours.

Heat the oil, 2 tablespoons of the butter, chiles (if using), cinnamon stick, cumin seeds, and saffron in a large pot over medium-high heat until the cinnamon unfurls, about 3 minutes. Add the beef and reduce the heat to medium-low, cooking until all sides of the meat are browned, 5 to 7 minutes.

Stir in the onions, potatoes, radishes, and garlic and cook for 6 minutes, stirring occasion-ally. Add the carrots and cook for 1 minute. Stir in the cumin, coriander, paprika, and 1 table-spoon of the salt and cook for 4 minutes, stirring occasionally.

Add the chopped tomatoes, scraping and stirring to work the browned bits at the bottom of the pot into the meat mixture. Cook for 2 minutes and then add the water and remaining 1 tablespoon of salt and bring to a boil. Reduce the heat to medium-low, cover, and simmer until the meat is fall-apart tender, 2 to 2½ hours. Stir in the remaining butter, taste for season-ing, and serve.

ZEYBA RAHMAN, an Indian woman who served as an adviser to the king of Morocco for the annual sacred music festival in Fez, invited me to the festival there many years ago. While there, I had the good fortune to dine at La Maison Bleue, a lovely Moorish-style hotel and restaurant run by Mehdi El Abbadi. They shared this amazing recipe for beef tagine with me. It's excellent served alongside couscous, mashed pota-toes, or leftover Chinese takeout rice. Cumin, one of my favorite spices, found its way to India from the Middle East and is also used a lot in Morocco. It lends a deep, almost smoky quality to the saucy meat stews, tagines, and braises.

CHAPTER 5

casseroles and one-dish dinners

Growing up in India, gathering together with friends and family for dinner was not reserved for special occasions but rather was an everyday occurrence. My family was known for entertaining guests with food and conversation, and at our table we discussed everything and anything, from politics to religion to the mundane details of our day at school and achievements on the playground. The discussions sometimes got heated and passionate. The only thing that could quell the unavoidable tumultuous turns was the power of delicious food. Food was the distraction that kept all of us in order without anyone having to play referee or moderator.

When I moved to New York City to go to art school in the early 1990s, it was only natural that I turned to food and entertaining as a way to meet and get to know people. Hosting dinner parties filled the void left by being far from my family and also served as a way to form strong and lasting friendships.

I discovered that the best way to get to know people was with a dinner invitation. My reputation for hosting elaborate dinner parties became legendary among my small circle of friends and acquaintances and when I moved from Manhattan to Brooklyn, I was even able to pull off a nearly impossible feat—inducing Manhattanites to cross the bridge for the promise of a great meal.

On these occasions, I almost always offered one of the dishes from this chapter. **I call them one-dish dinners because they offer protein and starch all in one.** While they are wonderful for feeding a family casserole-style, they also are great for entertaining and satisfying a hungry crowd.

Sometimes I made the dishes my friends and I were homesick for, like Imm Jaddara, a rice and lentil casserole, and Tahiree Rice Casserole, made with vegetables, which reminds me of the khitcheree that I ate as a child. Poha, which are pressed rice sticks that look like opaque rolled oats, is what I make when I crave something comforting and quick. Take the time to find an Indian market in your neighborhood and buy some poha. I guarantee you that the recipe for Shrimp Poha Paella will become a staple in your kitchen.

Other times, I lend an Indian inflection to dishes that I have sampled while traveling throughout the United States. In the recipe for Enchiladas, a roasted vegetable sauce, Stir-Fried Carrot Salad, and a modest sprinkling of cheese makes this dish unexpectedly fresh tasting and light, and in the recipe for Macaroni and Cheese, I employ the traditional Indian technique of gently frying spices in oil when making the cheese sauce. The Spinach Lasagna with Roasted Eggplant Sauce is a good choice for kids and vegetable-challenged adults, as it is packed with vegetables that get layered into the casserole as well as pureed in the sauce.

One-dish dinners are versatile. They can serve as the meal or as an element of a meal. Built on big flavors and often make-ahead friendly, these are the dishes that I return to time and again, whether for entertaining or for a family dinner. I hope that they serve as the groundwork for stimulating conversations and ironclad friendships at your table, too.

chicken and mixed sweet pepper pilaf (murgh pulao)

SERVES 6

Juice of 1 lemon
1 tablespoon ground coriander
½ teaspoon cayenne pepper
¼ teaspoon turmeric
Pinch of ground peppercorns
1½ pounds boneless, skinless chicken breasts and thighs, cut crosswise into ½-inch-wide strips
3 tablespoons canola oil
1½ teaspoons cumin seeds
1 large red onion, halved and sliced
A 2-inch piece fresh ginger, peeled and grated

1 red bell pepper, cored, seeded, and thinly sliced
1 yellow or orange bell pepper, cored, seeded, and thinly sliced
2 garlic cloves, peeled and finely chopped
1 jalapeño pepper (cored and seeded if you prefer a milder flavor), halved lengthwise and thinly sliced crosswise
1 tablespoon kosher salt
¾ cup chopped fresh cilantro
2 cups basmati rice
4 cups water

Mix the lemon juice, coriander, cayenne pepper, turmeric, and ground peppercorns in a medium bowl. Add the chicken, toss to coat, and set aside.

Heat the oil with the cumin seeds in a large pot or Dutch oven (preferably one with a lid) over medium-high heat until the cumin turns golden brown, about 2 minutes, stirring often. Add the onion and ginger and cook until the onion is soft, about 3 minutes, stirring often. Add the bell peppers, garlic, jalapeño, and salt and cook until the peppers soften slightly, 3 to 4 minutes, stirring occasionally.

Mix the cilantro in with the chicken and add to the pot with the peppers, cooking until the chicken is browned, about 4 to 6 minutes. Mix in the rice and fry for 2 minutes, stirring only once or twice. Add the water, bring to a boil, and cover. Reduce the heat to low and simmer for 20 minutes. Turn off the heat and serve.

AT ITS MOST BASIC, a biriyani is a layered rice pulao. They are laborious (some would say tedious) to make, so Indians cook them mostly for special occasions and celebrations. This chicken pilaf is much quicker to put together because the rice isn't cooked separately. I make it whenever I have to feed a large group of hungry friends, fast.

macaroni and cheese

SERVES 8 TO 10

1 pound pasta, such as penne, ziti, or elbows

1 pound Parmigiano-Reggiano cheese, coarsely grated

1 pound mixed soft to semihard cheeses, like Cheddar, Fontina, or Gouda, grated (about 6 cups)

4 ounces Pecorino cheese, coarsely grated

½ cup panko bread crumbs

4 tablespoons (½ stick) unsalted butter

1 teaspoon chopped fresh rosemary

1 teaspoon chopped fresh thyme

1 teaspoon ground peppercorns

¼ teaspoon red pepper flakes

2 tablespoons all-purpose flour

2 cups milk

1 tablespoon Dijon or spicy mustard

Preheat the oven to 400°F. Bring a large pot of salted water to a boil. When the water boils, add the pasta and cook until not quite al dente, 7 to 8 minutes; drain and set aside. Mix the grated cheeses together in a large bowl. Transfer ½ cup to a small bowl, mix with the bread crumbs, and set aside (this will be your topping).

Heat the butter with the rosemary, thyme, ground peppercorns, and pepper flakes in a large pot over medium-high heat until the herbs are fragrant and the butter is melted, stirring occasionally, 1 to 1½ minutes. Reduce the heat to medium, whisk in the flour, and cook for another minute. Drizzle in a couple of tablespoons of milk and whisk to combine. Once the milk is incorporated, add a couple more tablespoons and whisk in. Repeat until the flour paste is somewhat loose. Then add the remaining milk and whisk until smooth. Increase the heat to medium-high and cook, while stirring, until the sauce thickens slightly, 3½ to 4 minutes. Whisk in the mustard and cook another 30 seconds. Add the grated cheeses and stir until melted.

Stir the drained pasta into the sauce and transfer to a 3-quart casserole dish. Sprinkle with the bread crumb–cheese topping and bake until the topping is browned, 25 to 30 minutes. Serve immediately.

THIS IS SUCH a simple recipe for macaroni and cheese. Besides the Parmigiano-Reggiano, you can use whatever other cheeses you already have in your refrigerator; at my home, Cheddar, truffled Pecorino, nutty-sweet Mimolette, and Taleggio have all been incorporated into this recipe at one time or another. If using a strong cheese, like Taleggio or Gruyère, do so in moderation, adding no more than a quarter pound to the mix. With so much cheese in this recipe, you won't need to add extra salt.

baked ziti with vegetable sauce

SERVES 8 TO 10

FOR THE SAUCE

¼ cup extra-virgin olive oil plus
   1 teaspoon, for greasing baking dish
3 dried red chiles
½ teaspoon ground peppercorns
½ teaspoon chopped fresh rosemary
½ teaspoon chopped fresh thyme
1 large red onion, halved and thinly sliced
1 tablespoon kosher salt
2 red bell peppers, cored, seeded, and
   thinly sliced
1 tablespoon sugar
3 cups canned crushed tomatoes

FOR THE ZITI

1 pound mozzarella cheese, coarsely
   grated
8 ounces Parmigiano-Reggiano cheese,
   coarsely grated
4 ounces Pecorino cheese, coarsely grated
1 pound whole-milk or fat-free ricotta
   cheese
3 large eggs
1 cup chopped fresh basil leaves
2 tablespoons unsalted butter, melted,
   plus 2 tablespoons unsalted butter
½ teaspoon kosher salt
½ teaspoon ground peppercorns
1 pound ziti pasta

Preheat the oven to 400°F. Grease a 9 x 13-inch baking dish with 1 teaspoon of oil and set aside.

To make the sauce, heat the oil, chiles, and ground peppercorns in a large pot over medium-high heat, cooking until the chiles become slightly browned, about 1½ minutes. Add the rosemary and thyme, cook for 15 seconds, and then add the onion and salt and cook until onion is soft but not browned, stirring often, about 4 minutes. Reduce the heat to medium and add the bell peppers. Cook until they start to soften, stirring often, about 3 minutes. Mix in the sugar, reduce the heat to medium-low, cover the pot, and cook for 5 minutes, stirring halfway through. Add the tomatoes, bring to a boil, add 1 cup of water, and bring back to a boil. Reduce the heat to medium and partially cover the pot. Simmer for 20 minutes, stirring occasionally. Turn off the heat and set aside (at this point, the sauce can be refrigerated for up to 3 days, or frozen for up to 3 months).

To make the ziti, mix a quarter of the mozzarella, half of the Parmigiano-Reggiano, the Pecorino, ricotta, eggs, basil, melted butter, salt, and ground peppercorns together in a large bowl. Mix the remaining mozzarella and the remaining Parmesan cheese together in a small bowl.

Bring a large pot of salted water to a boil. Cook the pasta until al dente, drain, and add to the vegetable sauce along with 2 tablespoons of butter. Warm the sauce over medium-high heat and cook, stirring occasionally, until you can hear the sauce simmering at the bottom of the pot, about 2 minutes. Turn off the heat.

Add a third of the pasta to the baking dish. Divide the ricotta mixture into two equal portions and break marble-sized chunks off of one portion to dot over the pasta. Cover the ricotta with half of the remaining pasta, and then dot with the remaining mixture. Spread the rest of the pasta on top and sprinkle with the mozzarella-Parmesan mixture.

Bake the ziti until the cheese has melted and the sauce is bubbling around the edges of the baking dish, about 20 minutes. Turn the broiler to high and broil about 6 inches from the heating element until the top layer of cheese has browned, 2 to 3 minutes. Let the ziti stand for 5 minutes before serving.

MY AUNT RITA, who lives in upstate New York, made a baked ziti during my very first visit to the United States when I was in my teens. I combined this delicious memory with the recipe given to me by Jo Taibi, an Italian-American friend who wanted to show off what she considered to be the best baked casserole dish from her community. For a less rich dish, use fat-free ricotta in place of whole-milk ricotta. The sauce is so thick and flavorful that no one will miss the fat. This is wonderful with homemade garlic bread.

veggie enchiladas with roasted pepper sauce

SERVES 4 TO 6

1 tablespoon unsalted butter, at room
   temperature, for greasing
1 recipe Warm Roasted Pepper Dip
   (page 30)
8 (6-inch) whole-wheat tortillas
1/2 recipe Stir-Fried Carrot Salad (page 59)

1 cup shredded cheese (any combination
   of Cheddar, mozzarella, queso blanco,
   or Monterey Jack)
1/4 cup chopped fresh cilantro
Sour cream, for serving (optional)

Preheat the oven to 450°F. Grease the bottom of an 11 x 9-inch baking dish with butter, add
1/2 cup Warm Roasted Pepper Dip, and shake the dish to spread it evenly. Set the baking dish
aside.

Warm a griddle or medium nonstick skillet for 2 minutes over medium-high heat. Reduce
the heat to medium and warm each tortilla until it is pliable and smells toasty, about 15 to
20 seconds per side.

Roll a heaping 1/4 cup of the carrot salad in each tortilla and place seam side down in the
baking dish. Cover with the remaining dip and top with an even layer of cheese. Bake until the
cheese is melted and golden brown, about 20 minutes. Sprinkle with cilantro and serve with
sour cream (if using).

WITH THEIR LUSCIOUS roasted vegetable sauce and flavorful cabbage and
carrot filling, these Enchiladas are surprisingly light. A thin layer of cheese coats the
top, just enough to provide a browned, cheesy crust. They're creamy, spicy, and sweet,
a welcome change from the classic, heavy preparation. This is a great make-ahead meal
that can be assembled and frozen for up to 3 months. If using 8-inch instead of 6-inch
tortillas, add 1/3 cup of coleslaw to each tortilla.

imm jaddara

SERVES 8

10 cups water
½ cup extra-virgin olive oil
1½ teaspoons cumin seeds
½ teaspoon ground peppercorns
1 large red onion, quartered and sliced
   crosswise

2 tablespoons kosher salt
2 cups green French lentils
½ teaspoon Toasted Cumin (page 16)
¼ teaspoon cayenne pepper
1 cup basmati rice
1 lemon, cut into wedges, for serving

Place 1 cup of water next to your stovetop. Heat the oil with the cumin seeds and ground peppercorns in a large, wide, and heavy-bottomed pot over medium-high heat, cooking until the cumin is browned, about 2½ minutes. Add the onion and salt and cook until the onions are deep brown, stirring often, for 12 to 14 minutes. Once the onions start sticking to the bottom of the pot, splash them with water to keep them from sticking and burning, and scrape up the browned bits (you may not use all of the water).

   Pour in 2 cups of water and cook until most of the water is absorbed into the onions, 2 to 5 minutes. Stir in the lentils and fry until they're semidry and leave a trail when pushed across the bottom of the pot, stirring occasionally, for 2 minutes. Add 7 more cups of water, the Toasted Cumin, and cayenne pepper and bring to a boil. Reduce the heat to a moderate simmer and cook for 10 minutes. Add the rice, bring back to a boil, cover, and reduce the heat to medium-low. Cook until the lentils are slightly al dente and still remain whole, 35 to 40 minutes. Taste for seasoning and serve with lemon wedges.

I LEARNED HOW to make Imm Jaddara, a Lebanese lentil and rice dish, from my very good friend Mary Ann Joulwan. The onions are fried to a deep, toffee brown and give the lentils and rice a beautiful sweetness and gorgeous burnished color. I love this with fresh lemon juice added just before serving. Add a dollop of yogurt or Raita (page 18) and you have a complete protein. Sprinkle with thinly sliced fried shallots if you want to be really decadent.

tahiree rice casserole

SERVES 8

¼ cup canola oil
9 green cardamom pods
6 whole cloves
3 bay leaves
3 dried red chiles
1½ teaspoons cumin seeds
½ teaspoon whole black peppercorns
½ teaspoon ground peppercorns
½ teaspoon coriander seeds
1 large red onion, halved and sliced
2 tablespoons kosher salt

½ large head cauliflower, cut into florets (about 1¼ pounds)
2 medium red potatoes, peeled, cut into large chunks, and placed in a bowl of water
1 teaspoon turmeric
2 cups basmati rice
1½ cups frozen peas
½ teaspoon Garam Masala (page 20)
1 teaspoon Toasted Cumin (page 16)

Heat the oil with the cardamom pods, cloves, bay leaves, chiles, cumin seeds, whole peppercorns, ground peppercorns, and coriander in a large pot over medium-high heat. Cook until the cumin browns, stirring often, about 2½ minutes. Add the onion and half of the salt and cook until the onion just starts to soften, stirring occasionally, for about 2 minutes. Stir in the cauliflower, potatoes, and turmeric, reduce the heat to medium, and cook for 1 minute. Add the rice, cook for 1 minute, stirring occasionally, and then add the peas and 4 cups of water. Bring to a boil and then reduce the heat to low. Stir in the Garam Masala, Toasted Cumin, and remaining salt and cover. Cook for 20 minutes, then turn off the heat and let the Tahiree rest for 5 minutes. Fluff with a fork and serve.

WHEN I CRAVE comfort food fast, this is what I make. It's a marriage of two classic Indian dishes: khitcheree, a one-pot lentil and rice dish, and biriyani, a layered rice casserole. It's easy to make, too, since the vegetables are left in rustic chunks rather than chopped finely. Serve with Raita (page 18) or with Tomato Chutney (page 14).

spinach lasagna with roasted eggplant sauce

SERVES 8 TO 10

1 yellow summer squash
1 zucchini
3 medium carrots
2 eggplants (about 1 pound each), pricked 3 times with a fork
¼ cup extra-virgin olive oil
1 teaspoon ground peppercorns
¼ teaspoon red pepper flakes
½ teaspoon herbes de Provence
1 large red onion, chopped
1 tablespoon plus 2 teaspoons kosher salt
2 garlic cloves, peeled and minced

2 cups water
3¼ cups canned chopped tomatoes
1 (16-ounce) box lasagna noodles
2 tablespoons unsalted butter, at room temperature, for greasing
1½ pounds mozzarella cheese, coarsely grated
8 ounces Parmigiano-Reggiano cheese, coarsely grated
2 cups loosely packed fresh basil leaves
4 cups loosely packed baby spinach leaves

Adjust an oven rack so it is 6 inches from the broiler and preheat the broiler. Line a baking sheet with aluminum foil and roast the yellow squash, zucchini, carrots, and eggplants until they're charred on all sides, 20 to 30 minutes (10 to 15 minutes if roasting on the cooktop or on a cooktop grill), turning the vegetables with tongs every 5 minutes so they char evenly. Remove the vegetables as they are done (the smaller vegetables may be done before the eggplant) and set them aside to cool. Peel away as much of the charred skin as possible. Chop finely and set aside.

Heat the oil with the ground peppercorns, pepper flakes, and herbes de Provence in a large pot over medium-high heat until fragrant, about 2 minutes. Add the onion and salt and cook until the onion softens, stirring occasionally, for 3 to 4 minutes. Add the garlic and cook until it's fragrant, about 1 minute. Stir in the chopped roasted vegetables and their accumulated juices and cook, stirring often, for 5 minutes. Add 1 cup of the water and cook until it is absorbed into the vegetables. Add the tomatoes and the remaining water. Reduce the heat to medium and cook until the sauce is thick, about 15 minutes, stirring midway through.

Bring a large pot of salted water to a boil. Add the lasagna noodles and boil just until they're al dente, about 6 minutes. Drain the pasta, return it to the pot, cover with cold water, and set aside.

Preheat the oven to 400°F. Grease an extra-deep 13 x 9-inch lasagna pan with butter. Mix the mozzarella and Parmesan cheeses together in a small bowl and set aside. Place a layer of noodles in the bottom of the baking dish, slightly overlapping as you lay them in. Cover with a third of the sauce and half of the basil leaves. Cover with a third of the cheese mixture. Add another layer of pasta, half of the remaining sauce, and half of the remaining cheese. Arrange the spinach leaves in an even layer over the cheese. Add another layer of pasta, the rest of the sauce and top with the rest of the cheese. Tuck the remaining basil leaves into the cheese so the tips stick out. Bake until the top cheese layer is browned and bubbly, 20 to 30 minutes. Let the lasagna stand for 10 minutes before serving.

PEOPLE SOMETIMES tease me about my eating habits. "For a vegetarian you barely eat any vegetables," they say, and though I'm no longer a strict vegetarian, I do concede that my ideal meal consists of starch, starch, and more starch (if I could eat French fries for breakfast, lunch, and dinner, I would). That's why this lasagna is great— it packs tons of spinach and vegetables into a lusciously decadent casserole. After boiling the lasagna noodles, I submerge them in cold water so they don't stick together. If you don't have a deep 13 x 9-inch baking dish, you can use a 12 x 9-inch baking dish, but know that you'll only be able to fit in two layers of noodles and two-thirds of the sauce. You can char the vegetables over your cooktop instead of under your broiler— I sometimes use an iron roasting grate that fits over my stovetop and it works beautifully.

mushroom and rice biriyani casserole

SERVES 6 TO 8

FOR THE RICE
10 cups water
6 whole black peppercorns
4 whole cloves
4 green cardamom pods
2 bay leaves
A 1-inch piece cinnamon stick
2 cups basmati rice

FOR THE CASSEROLE
¼ cup canola oil
6 whole black peppercorns
6 green cardamom pods
3 whole cloves
1 tablespoon mustard seeds

1 teaspoon cumin seeds
36 curry leaves, roughly torn (optional)
1 to 6 dried red chiles (optional)
1 teaspoon turmeric
1 teaspoon ground coriander
2 pounds white button mushrooms,
    trimmed and thickly sliced
1 tablespoon kosher salt
1 teaspoon Sambhaar (page 21),
    or ½ teaspoon curry powder
1 cup buttermilk, well shaken
¼ teaspoon ground peppercorns
1 tablespoon softened unsalted butter
¾ cup chopped fresh cilantro
½ cup water

Bring the water to a boil in a large pot with the whole peppercorns, cloves, cardamom pods, bay leaves, and cinnamon. Stir the rice and return to a boil, then reduce the heat to a vigorous simmer. Cook, partially covered, for 6 minutes. Drain and set aside (you can pick out the whole spices if you like).

Preheat the oven to 350°F. To make the casserole, heat the oil, whole peppercorns, cardamom, cloves, mustard seeds, and cumin seeds in a large skillet or wok over medium-high heat, cooking until the cumin is browned and the mustard seeds start to pop, 1½ to 2½ minutes. Add the curry leaves (if using), chiles (if using), and turmeric and cook, stirring often, for 1 minute. Reduce the heat to low, add the coriander, and cook while stirring, until the chiles start to darken, about 1 minute. Add the mushrooms and salt to the skillet and increase the heat to medium-high (the skillet will be full at this point). Cook, stirring often, until the mushrooms release their liquid and their total volume is reduced by about half, 4 to 5 minutes. Mix in the Sambhaar and then stir in the buttermilk. Bring to a vigorous simmer and cook until the liquid is reduced by half and slightly thick, 8 to 12 minutes (there will still be quite a bit of sauce). Stir in the ground peppercorns and turn off the heat.

Grease a 10-cup oven-safe casserole dish or Dutch oven (preferably one with a lid) with butter. Add 2 cups of the cooked rice, spreading it evenly over the bottom of the dish. Cover with half of the mushroom mixture and sprinkle with a third of the cilantro. Evenly spread 1½ cups of rice over the cilantro and cover with the remaining mushrooms and half of the remaining cilantro. Evenly spread the remaining rice on top and pour the water around the edges of the dish. Cover tightly with aluminum foil, seal with a lid, and bake for 35 minutes. Remove the casserole from the oven and let it stand covered for 10 minutes. Uncover, sprinkle with the remaining cilantro, and serve.

THIS IS A VEGETARIAN biriyani purely of my own invention. It is unusual that it contains no onions or tomatoes; its flavor is based solely on mushrooms and a southern Indian palette of spices. For a more substantial meal, add a can of drained chickpeas to the mushroom mixture. Serve this as a main coarse with Raita (page 18) or as a side dish. In India, we leave the whole spices in the final dish, but if you prefer, you can pick out the whole spices before layering the rice into the casserole.

shrimp poha paella

SERVES 8

2 pounds large or extra-large shrimp,
  peeled and deveined
Juice of ½ lemon plus ½ lemon, cut into
  wedges
1 tablespoon plus 1 teaspoon kosher salt
1½ teaspoons turmeric
¼ teaspoon ground peppercorns
4 tablespoons (½ stick) unsalted butter
24 curry leaves, roughly torn (optional)
1 tablespoon mustard seeds

1½ teaspoons cumin seeds
1 large red onion, quartered and thinly
  sliced crosswise
1½ cups frozen peas
¼ teaspoon cayenne pepper
4 cups poha, rinsed in cold water and
  drained
½ cup water
½ cup chopped fresh cilantro
Lemon wedges, for serving

Place the shrimp in a large bowl and mix them with the lemon juice, 1 teaspoon of salt, ¾ teaspoon of the turmeric, and the ground peppercorns; set aside.

Melt the butter with the curry leaves (if using), mustard seeds, and cumin seeds in a large pot or wok over medium-high heat, stirring often, until the cumin begins to darken, 2 to 3 minutes. Add the onion, the remaining ¾ teaspoon turmeric, and remaining tablespoon of salt and cook, stirring occasionally, for 5 minutes. Add the frozen peas and cook for 2 minutes, then add the shrimp and cook for an additional 2 minutes. Stir in the cayenne pepper and poha and cook for 1½ minutes. Drizzle the water around the edges of the pot, reduce the heat to medium-low, cover, and cook for 7 minutes. Remove the cover and fluff. Taste for seasoning and sprinkle with the chopped cilantro. Serve with lemon wedges.

POHA RICE PASTA is the Indian version of instant Uncle Ben's. Made by pressing grains of rice flat, it is a wonder starch that cooks quickly, like couscous, but has a beautiful fluffy lightness that is incomparable to any other starch. I grew up eating Potato-and-Pea Poha (page 217) for breakfast and also took it as tiffin to school. With poha in your cupboard and shrimp in your freezer, you can make this meal in 20 minutes. If you don't have an Indian market nearby, you can order poha from the resources on page 253.

lamb and spinach phyllo bake (keema)

SERVES 8

1 cup bulgur

2 cups plus 2 tablespoons water

1½ pounds baby spinach

1 cup tightly packed fresh cilantro

½ cup tightly packed fresh basil leaves

¼ cup canola oil

12 green cardamom pods

6 whole cloves

2 teaspoons cumin seeds

A 2-inch piece cinnamon stick

½ teaspoon whole black peppercorns

1 red onion, finely chopped

1 jalapeño (cored and seeded if you prefer a milder flavor), finely chopped

1½ tablespoons kosher salt

A ½-inch piece fresh ginger, peeled and grated

3 garlic cloves, peeled and finely chopped

½ teaspoon ground cumin

1 teaspoon ground coriander

2 pounds ground lamb

½ cup plain yogurt

1 teaspoon Garam Masala (page 20)

1 stick plus 1 tablespoon unsalted butter

1 package phyllo dough

Preheat the oven to 425°F. Place the bulgur in a medium pot. Add 2 cups of water and bring to a boil. Reduce the heat to low, cover, and simmer for 5 minutes. Turn off the heat and set aside, covered.

Bring a large pot of water to a boil. Add the spinach, cilantro, and basil and blanch just until they're wilted, about 30 seconds. Drain and place under cold running water then squeeze out some water (don't wring completely dry). Place the greens in your food processor with 2 table-spoons of water and process until you have a thick puree, adding more water if necessary. Set aside.

Heat the oil with the cardamom pods, cloves, cumin seeds, cinnamon stick, and whole peppercorns in a large skillet or wok over medium-high heat until the cinnamon unfurls and the spices are toasted, 2½ to 3 minutes, stirring occasionally. Add the onion, jalapeño, and salt and cook until the onion is soft, about 3 minutes, stirring occasionally. Add the ginger and garlic and cook until fragrant, about 1 minute, stirring often, and then add the ground cumin and coriander and cook for 30 seconds. Mix in the bulgur and the lamb and cook, stirring often, until the lamb turns pale, about 5 minutes.

Mix in half of the yogurt, cook 30 seconds, and then add the remaining yogurt and cook until the liquid is absorbed and the grains get a little clumpy when stirred, 1½ to 2 minutes. Add ½ teaspoon of the Garam Masala and cook 30 seconds. Add the spinach puree and cook for 2 minutes, stirring often. Turn off the heat and transfer the mixture to a large bowl.

Melt the butter in the microwave or in a small saucepan and stir in the remaining ½ tea-spoon of Garam Masala. Grease a 9 x 12-inch baking dish with a little melted butter and carefully lay 1 sheet of phyllo in the baking dish. Brush with some butter. Add another sheet of phyllo and brush with butter. Repeat three times, brushing each sheet with butter before covering with the next sheet. Gently spread a third of the filling over the phyllo. Top with 3 more sheets of phyllo, brushing each sheet with butter before covering with the next sheet. Add half of the remaining lamb mixture and top with 3 more sheets of phyllo, again brushing each sheet with butter before covering with the next. Add the remaining lamb mixture and top with the remaining sheets of phyllo, brushing each sheet with butter before covering with the next sheet. Brush the top of the last sheet with the remaining butter. Using a sharp paring knife, cut through all of the phyllo and lamb layers to make eight even rectangles. Bake for 35 to 45 minutes, or until the phyllo is golden brown and crisp. Remove and let cool for at least 10 minutes before serving. Serve hot or at room temperature.

VARIATION: Keema-Stuffed Samosas

Lay a sheet of frozen and thawed puff pastry on a lightly floured work surface. Cut the sheet into thirds along the lines of the folds. Roll out one third to a 6 x 12-inch rectangle. Cut the rectangle crosswise into thirds to make three smaller rectangles. Brush all around the edges of each with egg glaze (1 egg yolk beaten with a pinch of salt). Spoon a generous tablespoon of keema in the center. Fold the top of the rectangle down so it meets the bottom layer 1 to 1½ inches above the bottom edge and makes a triangle. Fold the bottom up and tuck the overhang over. Press gently to seal. Place on a baking sheet and brush with egg glaze. Repeat. Bake until crisp, 18 to 20 minutes. Serve hot. **MAKES 9 SAMOSAS**

KEEMA IS A TRADITIONAL dish for Indians who eat meat. It's incredibly versatile. In this recipe I layer it with phyllo dough, but you can serve it solo with warmed pita or crusty bread, or use it as a stuffing for mini pitas, samosas, or empanadas. In India it is commonplace to add yogurt to meat dishes. It tenderizes and adds a tangy flavor as well as introduces protein and healthy bacteria to the body. You can make this with chewier farro instead of bulgur if you like—bring it to a boil with 2 inches of water, boil for 5 minutes, and drain. Then add 2 beaten eggs to the mixture before layering it with the phyllo.

haleem "chili"

SERVES 8

3 medium red onions, quartered, plus
   ½ red onion, thinly sliced, for serving
4 garlic cloves, peeled and roughly
   chopped
A 2-inch piece fresh ginger, peeled and
   roughly chopped
1 or 2 jalapeños (cored and seeded if you
   prefer a milder flavor), roughly chopped
7½ cups water
¼ cup plus 2 tablespoons canola oil
12 green cardamom pods
6 whole cloves
3 dried red chiles

1½ teaspoons cumin seeds
A 1-inch piece cinnamon stick
1 teaspoon coriander seeds
¼ teaspoon whole black peppercorns
2 tablespoons kosher salt
2 teaspoons ground coriander
1 teaspoon ground cumin
½ teaspoon turmeric
2 pounds ground beef (preferably
   85% lean)
1 cup steel-cut oats
Chopped fresh cilantro, for serving
Lime wedges, for serving

Place the quartered onions, garlic, ginger, and jalapeños in the bowl of a food processor, pulse to a coarse puree, and set aside.

Place ½ cup of water next to your stovetop. Heat ¼ cup canola oil with the cardamom pods, cloves, chiles, cumin seeds, cinnamon, coriander seeds, and whole peppercorns in a large pot over medium-high heat until the cinnamon unfurls, 2 to 2½ minutes. Add the pureed onion mixture and salt and cook for 15 minutes, stirring often, scraping up the browned bits from the bottom of the pot and splashing the pot with water when the onions begin to stick.

Add the ground coriander, ground cumin, and turmeric and cook for 1 minute. Mix in 2 tablespoons of canola oil, the ground beef, oats, and 4 cups of water. Bring to a boil and reduce the heat to a simmer, cooking until the pot is fairly dry, 10 to 15 minutes. Add 3 more cups of water and bring back to a boil. Reduce the heat, cover, and simmer for 40 minutes, stirring every 10 minutes. Remove the lid and cook for 5 additional minutes. Serve with sliced onions, cilantro, and lime wedges.

HALEEM IS FAVORED by northern India's Muslim community, but you can find it nearly everywhere, from restaurants to street vendors who offer it with naan to the laborers and revelers who eat side by side late at night on Bombay's Muhammed Ali Road. I learned to make Haleem from Naushab Ahmed, one of my closest friends, and a great host. Made with ground beef and served in bowls, it gets topped with accoutrements like sliced onions, chopped green chiles, and fresh cilantro—not too dissimilar from chili. To vary the recipe's flavor and texture, you can substitute ¾ cup of yellow split peas or 1 cup of rice for the steel-cut oats if you like.

fish and shellfish

I have never heard more superlatives used around fish than when in the company of people from West Bengal or Bangladesh, where machar jhol (fish curry) and shorsha maach (mustard-flavored fish) are prepared and consumed as enthusiastically as are burgers and pizza here in the States. Bengal is just one of many fish-friendly states in India, a society to which Kerala, Goa, and Maharashtra also belong. India has an incredible breadth and variety of fish to choose from, like surmai (kingfish), kekra (crab), and bangda (mackerel). Those of us who have made new homes in America have become masters of substitution, and though the names of the fish may change, the rules of the game hold firm: Always use the freshest fish available and never, ever, compromise on quality.

Even though we buy our fish at a supermarket and not from fishermen (unless we're very lucky seacoast dwellers or have access to fishermen at farmers' markets), freshness and quality should still guide us in choosing the best specimens from the seafood case. Generally speaking, if the fish smells like the sea (or in the case of freshwater fish, it smells fresh, like rain), has clear and bright eyes, healthy-looking gills, and is very firm and taut to the touch, feel confident in your decision to buy it. If it doesn't meet these criteria, a little flexibility comes in handy. If the cod looks dull, reach for a glistening fillet of hake, haddock, or ocean perch. If the salmon looks soft or smells fishy, ask instead for Arctic char, halibut, or responsibly caught swordfish. Substitute clams for the mussels in the Double-Basil Mussels with Pasta Shells, or freshwater trout for flounder in the Fried Flounder Bites. Be empowered and excited by your options, not enslaved by an ingredient list.

You'll notice that in many of this chapter's recipes the fish and shellfish marinate in a citrus and salt brine while other ingredients are prepared. This is a great way to cleanse fish, making it receptive to any of the flavors and spices you'll introduce it to later. Leaving fish a little rare rather than cooking it completely further allows the flavors that you marinated it with to come forward.

The elegance of a beautiful fish dish is unrivaled in the world of food. With little effort, any meal becomes special with its addition. If purchased wisely and handled carefully, fish and shellfish can be amazing partners to most all kinds of sauces and marinades. Whether baked, fried, steamed, braised, or grilled, fish and shellfish deserve to be repeat guests at your dinner table.

twice-marinated halibut
with cilantro pesto

SERVES 4

FOR THE MARINADE
2 garlic cloves, peeled and chopped
1 teaspoon kosher salt
1 teaspoon ground peppercorns
2 tablespoons lemon juice (from about
⅟₂ lemon)

4 halibut fillets (about 6 ounces each)

FOR THE SAUCE
2 garlic cloves, peeled and roughly
chopped
15 curry leaves (optional)

A ⅟₂-inch piece fresh ginger, peeled and
roughly chopped
1 cup fresh cilantro, roughly chopped
1 teaspoon kosher salt
1½ teaspoons white wine vinegar
1 teaspoon balsamic vinegar
2 tablespoons extra-virgin olive oil
2 tablespoons coconut milk

Canola oil, for broiling
Kosher salt
1 lemon, cut into wedges, for serving

To make the marinade, place all of the ingredients in a gallon-sized resealable plastic bag and shake to mix. Add the halibut and turn to coat. Refrigerate for at least 30 minutes, or up to 2 hours.

To make the sauce, combine all of the ingredients in a food processor and pulse until they are completely smooth. Move an oven rack to the upper-middle position. Preheat the broiler and line a rimmed baking sheet with aluminum foil.

Place the halibut on the prepared baking sheet, skin side down, and make two diagonal slits cutting midway into the center of the fillet. Coat each fillet with some of the herb sauce, making sure that the sauce gets into the slits. Drizzle some canola oil over the top of each fillet and broil until the sauce on the surface is bubbling and the fillets are opaque in the middle (if using thick fillets, flip them halfway through cooking and drizzle with more oil; if using thin fillets, there's no need to flip them), 10 to 12 minutes. Sprinkle with salt and serve with lemon wedges.

THIS FISH DISH is popular all over Goa, where Portuguese ingredients—in this case vinegar (though perhaps not balsamic)—have influenced the food for hundreds of years. Traditionally the fish is grilled, but I find broiling it just as delicious, and easier during New York winters. You can substitute cod, haddock, tilapia, or any mild, flaky whitefish. If you don't have a couple of tablespoons of coconut milk handy for the sauce, feel free to increase the quantity of canola oil to a quarter cup; and if you don't have fresh curry leaves, substitute fresh basil instead—the sauce will still be absolutely delicious. This recipe can be easily doubled to serve eight.

salmon "en papillote" with tomato chutney

SERVES 6

2¼ cups Better-Than-Ketchup Tomato
  Chutney (page 14)
6 salmon fillets (6 to 8 ounces each), any
  small bones removed with tweezers

1 tablespoon kosher salt
1 teaspoon ground peppercorns
Chopped fresh cilantro, for serving
Lemon or lime wedges, for serving

Preheat the oven to 450°F. Cut six pieces of aluminum foil about 15 inches long and place them on your work surface. Add 3 tablespoons Tomato Chutney to the center of each piece of foil and place a fillet on top skin-side down. Season each piece of salmon with salt and ground peppercorns and top with another 3 tablespoons of chutney.

Bring both long sides of the foil up over the salmon and fold the edges over twice to seal (allow some space to remain between the top of the salmon and the foil—the foil should not be flush to the fish). Fold up the short ends of the foil, completely sealing the salmon within the foil package.

Place all of the packages on a rimmed baking sheet and roast for 10 minutes. Remove the baking sheet from the oven and open one package to see if the salmon is cooked to your preferred degree of doneness by flaking the center of the fillet with a paring knife or fork; if it is too rare, simply refold the package and let sit for a couple of minutes. The heat within the package will continue to cook the fillet, even though it is out of the oven. When the fish is cooked to your liking, unfold or cut open the packets, slide the fish and sauce out, sprinkle with cilantro, and serve with lemon or lime wedges.

WHEN CREATING THE SALMON packages, remember that they don't need to look perfect. The idea is to seal the salmon within the foil, allowing enough room in the package to accommodate the steam that is generated, which cooks the fish. If you can make the package look nice and neat, consider it a bonus.

coconut-braised salmon

SERVES 6

FOR THE MARINADE

¼ cup lemon juice (from about 1 lemon),
  or ¼ cup lime juice (from about 2 limes)

½ teaspoon Sambhaar (page 21) or curry
  powder

2 teaspoons kosher salt

1 teaspoon ground peppercorns

6 salmon fillets (6 ounces each), any small
  bones removed with tweezers

FOR THE SAUCE

2 tablespoons canola oil

30 curry leaves, roughly torn

1 to 6 dried red chiles (optional)

1 tablespoon plus 1 teaspoon mustard
  seeds

2 teaspoons cumin seeds

1 teaspoon ground peppercorns

2 medium red onions, finely chopped

2 tablespoons plus 2 teaspoons kosher
  salt

6 medium tomatoes, finely chopped

2 cups coconut milk

2 tablespoons canola oil

½ cup chopped fresh cilantro

Place the marinade ingredients in a gallon-sized resealable plastic bag. Add the salmon and turn to coat. Refrigerate for 30 minutes, or up to overnight (note that salmon marinated overnight will cook faster).

Preheat the oven to 400°F. To make the sauce, heat the canola oil with the curry leaves, chiles (if using), mustard seeds, cumin seeds, and ground peppercorns in a large skillet over medium-high heat for 2 minutes or until the mustard seeds begin to pop. Add the onions and salt and cook, stirring often, until the onions are soft and just beginning to brown, 5 to 8 minutes. Add the tomatoes and cook, stirring occasionally, until they break down and the sauce thickens, about 10 minutes. Stir in the coconut milk and bring to a simmer. Transfer to a large baking dish.

Heat the canola oil in a large skillet over high heat until it shimmers and is hot, 2½ minutes. Add 3 to 4 salmon fillets, skin side down, and sear until browned, 2 to 3 minutes. Place the salmon skin side on top of the sauce in the baking dish, taking care not to overlap the fillets. Repeat with the remaining salmon fillets. Bake the salmon until it is opaque at its edges and nearly cooked through to the center, 12 to 15 minutes (if the fillets are thin, reduce baking time to 10 to 12 minutes). Remove the salmon from the oven, sprinkle with cilantro, and serve skin side down with plenty of sauce.

TECHNICALLY, THE SALMON in this dish isn't braised—but the thickness and richness of the sauce reminds me of the kind of intense, thick sauce that develops during braising. The coconut milk in the sauce tempers the sharpness of the chiles and provides a sweet richness that isn't as heavy as a sauce made with dairy.

fried flounder bites

2 tablespoons lime juice (from about
   1 lime)
1 teaspoon kosher salt
½ teaspoon ground peppercorns
6 flounder fillets (6 to 8 ounces each), cut
   into 2-inch-wide strips

FOR THE MARINADE
⅓ cup sour cream
3 garlic cloves, peeled and finely minced
¼ teaspoon ground cumin
¾ teaspoon ground coriander
¾ teaspoon turmeric
½ teaspoon paprika

¼ teaspoon cayenne pepper
¼ teaspoon Garam Masala (page 20)
1 teaspoon kosher salt
½ teaspoon ground peppercorns
2½ tablespoons lime juice (from about
   1 lime)

Canola oil, for frying
24 curry leaves (optional)
1 lime cut into wedges, for serving
Green Chutney (page 8), Tamarind
   Chutney (page 13), or Raita (page 18), for
   serving

Place the lime juice, salt, and pepper together in a gallon-sized resealable plastic bag. Add the fish, turn to coat, and set aside.

To make the marinade, whisk all of the ingredients together in a large bowl. Pour the marinade into the plastic bag and let the fish marinate for 20 minutes, or up to 1 hour.

Fill a deep pot or wok with 2 inches of canola oil and heat it to 375°F. Carefully add 4 to 6 pieces of fish (avoid overcrowding the pot, which reduces the temperature of the oil). Fry for 2 minutes, add 4 curry leaves (if using), turn the fish, and continue to fry until the fish is browned, 1 to 3 minutes longer. Remove the fish and curry leaves from the oil and place on a paper towel–lined plate. Let the oil come back up to 375°F before frying the next batch. Repeat until all of the fish and curry leaves are fried. Serve with lime wedges and Green Chutney, Tamarind Chutney, or Raita.

I MARINATE FLOUNDER to give it extra flavor and then fry without a batter at a very high heat to brown it while keeping it delicate and light textured. Let the flounder rest in salt, pepper, and lime juice while you prepare the marinade. This step gives the fish a nice, fresh flavor.

goan-style shrimp curry

SERVES 8

FOR THE MARINADE
½ teaspoon kosher salt
¼ teaspoon ground peppercorns
¼ teaspoon cayenne pepper
2 tablespoons lemon juice (from about
    ½ lemon)

1 pound large or extra-large shrimp,
    peeled and deveined

FOR THE SAUCE
1 cup water
¼ cup canola oil
24 curry leaves, roughly torn (optional)

4 dried red chiles
1 teaspoon ground peppercorns
A 3-inch piece ginger, peeled and minced
1 medium red onion, finely chopped
1 tablespoon plus 1 teaspoon kosher salt
2 garlic cloves, peeled and chopped
2 teaspoons ground coriander
½ teaspoon turmeric
2 cups canned chopped tomatoes
1 teaspoon Sambhaar (page 21),
    or ½ teaspoon curry powder
1½ cups coconut milk
1 cup chopped fresh cilantro

To make the marinade, place all of the ingredients in a gallon-sized resealable plastic bag. Add the shrimp, toss to coat, and refrigerate.

Set ½ cup of water next to the stovetop. Heat the oil with the curry leaves (if using) and chiles in a medium pot over medium-high heat until the curry leaves start to sizzle, 1 to 2 minutes. Add the ground peppercorns and cook for 1 minute longer. Stir in the ginger, onion, and salt and cook, stirring often, until the onion is browned, about 8 minutes, sprinkling with water and stirring whenever the onion and ginger begin to stick to the bottom of the pot.

Add the garlic, coriander, and turmeric and cook until the garlic is fragrant, about 1 minute. Reduce the heat to medium-low and add the tomatoes to the pot. Cook, stirring and scraping the browned bits up from the sides and bottom of the pot, for 1 minute. Increase the heat to medium-high and simmer for 5 minutes, stirring often. Stir in the Sambhaar and cook for 1 minute, and then pour in the coconut milk and ½ cup of water. Bring to a boil and add the shrimp and any accumulated juices. Bring to a simmer and cook until the shrimp are curled and opaque, about 2 minutes. Stir in the cilantro and serve.

EACH REGION of the western coast of India has its own favorite shrimp curry, with no two cooks—even those who live on the same block—ever making the same recipe or revealing their family's secret. This recipe is inspired by a wonderful version that I had at a friend's home in Goa. Sambhaar, especially when homemade, gives the sauce an amazing depth of flavor. There are times when I crave just the sauce of this curry so I make it without the shrimp and eat it with lots of rice.

shrimp scampi masala

SERVES 6 TO 8

¼ cup lemon juice (from about 1 lemon)

2 teaspoons kosher salt

2 pounds large or extra-large shrimp, peeled and deveined

12 scallions (white and light green parts only), thinly sliced

1 cup fresh cilantro, chopped

½ teaspoon ground peppercorns

8 ounces capellini or angel hair pasta or thickly sliced rustic Italian bread (grilled, toasted, or broiled if you like), for serving

¼ cup ghee or clarified butter

3 dried red chiles

12 garlic cloves (about 1 head), peeled and finely minced

Place the lemon juice and salt in a gallon-sized resealable plastic bag. Add the shrimp and toss to coat. Refrigerate for 15 to 30 minutes and then add the scallions, cilantro, and ground peppercorns and set aside.

If serving the shrimp with pasta, bring a large pot of salted water to a boil. Add the pasta, cook until al dente, drain, and set aside.

While the pasta boils, cook the shrimp. Heat the ghee or clarified butter with the chiles in a large skillet or wok over medium-high heat until the chiles start to sizzle, 1 to 2 minutes. Add the garlic and cook until fragrant, stirring often, for 1 minute. Add the shrimp and cook until curled and opaque, 2 to 4 minutes, stirring often so the garlic doesn't stick to the bottom of the skillet. Toss the shrimp with pasta or divide among bowls if serving with bread, taste for seasoning, and serve.

REDOLENT WITH GARLIC, this scampi isn't heavy at all but rather fresh tasting from sliced scallions and lots of cilantro. Dried red chiles add spice, while ghee, the clarified butter of the subcontinent, introduces a delicious richness. If you can't find ghee, substitute clarified butter: Melt 7 tablespoons unsalted butter in the microwave in a glass measuring cup. Let the butter cool until the milk solids sink to the bottom and then spoon the golden liquid butter from the top, leaving the white solids behind. While pasta is the traditional accompaniment to scampi, a few slabs of crusty Italian bread are also fitting.

lobster with cilantro butter

SERVES 4

1½ cups (3 sticks) unsalted butter, softened

6 garlic cloves, peeled and roughly chopped

⅓ cup fresh cilantro

¼ cup fresh mint leaves

2 lemons, zested and quartered, for serving

½ teaspoon sugar

2½ teaspoons kosher salt

1 teaspoon ground peppercorns

4 cooked lobsters, about 1½-pounds each

Set an oven rack at the upper-middle position and preheat the broiler. Line a rimmed baking sheet with aluminum foil and set aside.

Place the butter, garlic, cilantro, mint, lemon zest, sugar, salt, and ground peppercorns in a food processor and process until smooth.

Set the lobsters on your work surface and split in half lengthwise. Loosen the meat from the tail section, leaving it in the shell, and place the tail on the prepared baking sheet. Crack the claws and remove the meat, laying the meat on top of the body and head. Spread the meat and tail with the cilantro butter and broil until sizzling and starting to brown, 3 to 5 minutes. Remove the lobsters from the baking sheet and arrange on a platter. Pour pooled butter from the baking sheet into individual ramekins and serve alongside the lobster with lemon wedges.

THE IDEA FOR THIS DISH came to me while I was visiting Sri Lanka. The fish markets had all been decimated by the 2005 tsunami, so the local fishermen arranged their day's catch at roadside stands. Young divers routinely appeared with the most pristine fresh lobsters. I bought some lobsters one afternoon and gave them to the chef in the home where I was staying. He prepared them with these flavors. Because it is made with cooked lobsters, this is a simple, quick dish with great looks and lots of snob appeal. If you prefer, you can of course purchase live lobsters and cook them as you like, and then proceed with the recipe.

double-basil mussels with pasta shells

SERVES 8

1 pound conchiglie pasta shells or other pasta shape

2 pounds mussels, debearded and scrubbed

3 tablespoons extra-virgin olive oil

1 cup fresh basil leaves, a third roughly chopped

¼ teaspoon red pepper flakes

1 teaspoon ground peppercorns

3 garlic cloves, peeled and roughly chopped

3 cups canned chopped tomatoes

1 tablespoon kosher salt

Bring a large pot of salted water to a boil. Add the pasta, cook until al dente, then drain and set aside. While the pasta boils, cook the mussels.

Heat the oil, chopped basil, pepper flakes, and ground peppercorns in a large skillet or pot over medium-high heat for 2 minutes. Add the garlic and cook until fragrant, about 1 minute. Add the mussels, cook for 30 seconds, and then cover the skillet. Reduce the heat to medium-low and cook until all of the mussels open, 3 to 4 minutes. (Discard any that do not open.)

Using a slotted spoon, remove the mussels from the skillet to a bowl and set aside. Stir the tomatoes and salt into the skillet and bring to a boil. Reduce the heat to a simmer and cook until slightly thickened, about 4 minutes. Add the mussels and any accumulated juices back to the skillet along with the cooked pasta and whole basil leaves, and use tongs to toss everything together. Cover the skillet, cook for 1 minute to combine the flavors, and serve.

FAST, FRESH, AND SIMPLE, this mussels-and-pasta dinner can be on the table in 20 minutes. The sauce is infused with basil twice: In the beginning it is fried with the ground peppercorns and at the end it is added fresh with the mussels. Frying fresh and dried herbs and spices is an Indian culinary trick that adds depth and an extra layer of intensity to just about any dish.

scallops with roasted pepper chutney

SERVES 8

FOR THE SCALLOPS
½ cup extra-virgin olive oil
2 garlic cloves, peeled and finely chopped
A 2-inch piece fresh ginger, peeled and
    finely chopped
1 teaspoon cayenne pepper
16 large scallops

FOR THE CHUTNEY
4 red bell peppers
1 medium red onion

A 1-inch piece fresh ginger
¼ cup heavy cream
2 tablespoons lime juice (from about
    1 lime)
1 tablespoon plus 1½ teaspoons kosher
    salt
½ teaspoon Toasted Cumin (page 16)
½ teaspoon ground peppercorns
½ teaspoon Garam Masala (page 20)
¼ teaspoon cayenne pepper
1½ tablespoons ghee or clarified butter

To prepare the scallops, place the oil, garlic, ginger, and cayenne pepper in a gallon-sized resealable plastic bag. Add the scallops and turn to coat. Refrigerate the scallops while you make the chutney.

Set an oven rack at the upper-middle position and preheat the broiler. Prepare the chutney: Place the peppers, onion, and ginger on an aluminum foil–lined baking sheet and broil for 15 minutes, turning often, until all sides of the vegetables and ginger are charred (you may need to remove the ginger before the peppers and onion are finished). Place them in a large bowl and cover with plastic wrap for 30 minutes. Peel the charred skin from the peppers and onion and trim the blackened skin from the ginger. Place the roasted and peeled vegetables and ginger in a food processor along with the heavy cream, lime juice, salt, Toasted Cumin, ground peppercorns, Garam Masala, and cayenne pepper and pulse until smooth.

Warm a large skillet over medium-high heat for 2 minutes. Add the ghee and heat for 1 minute. Add enough scallops to fill the skillet and cook on one side without moving until they're browned, about 1½ minutes. Flip the scallops and cook the other side until browned, about 1 minute longer. Place the scallops on a large serving dish. Cover with foil to keep warm while you cook the remaining scallops. When all of the scallops are browned, discard all but 2 tablespoons of fat from the skillet and add the chutney. Bring it to a boil, reduce the heat to medium-low, and simmer for 2 minutes. Taste the chutney for seasoning, pour over the scallops, and serve.

THE DIFFERENCE BETWEEN melted butter and ghee or clarified butter is that melted unsalted butter still contains milk solids. If you heat butter for a long time or at a high temperature, these milk solids can burn and make food bitter. The milk solids are removed from the ghee and clarified butter, so they can be heated for a long time and at relatively high temperatures without any risk of burning. The resulting flavor is rich and nutty, a more complex and elegant flavor than could ever be achieved with plain unsalted butter. It really brings out the natural richness of the scallops.

bombay-style whole snapper

SERVES 4

6 tablespoons extra-virgin olive oil

1 whole red snapper (2½ to 3 pounds), cleaned and scaled

½ cup lemon juice (from about 2 lemons) plus 1 lemon, cut into wedges

48 fresh or frozen curry leaves (optional)

6 whole cloves

5 green cardamom pods

3 dried red chiles (optional)

3 tablespoons coriander seeds

2 tablespoons cumin seeds

2 tablespoons mustard seeds

½ teaspoon whole peppercorns

2 tablespoons water

6 garlic cloves, peeled and roughly chopped

1 jalapeño (cored and seeded if you prefer a milder flavor), roughly chopped

1 cup loosely packed fresh cilantro

¼ cup loosely packed fresh mint leaves

2 tablespoons kosher salt

¼ teaspoon ground ginger

¼ teaspoon ground mace

⅛ teaspoon ground allspice

Grease a baking dish large enough to hold the fish comfortably with 2 tablespoons of oil. Place the snapper on your work surface and make three or four diagonal gashes in the fish, holding a paring or boning knife nearly parallel to the flesh so the gash opens like a flap. Sprinkle the fish with 2 tablespoons of lemon juice. Flip the fish over and repeat on the other side. Set aside.

Heat the curry leaves (if using), cloves, cardamom pods, chiles (if using), coriander seeds, cumin seeds, mustard seeds, and peppercorns in a medium skillet over medium-high heat for 2 minutes, stirring occasionally. Reduce the heat to medium and toast until the cumin seeds are medium brown in color and the mustard seeds start to pop, 1½ to 2 minutes. Transfer the spices to a spice grinder, coffee mill, or small food processor and grind until fine.

Transfer the spice blend to a food processor. Add 4 tablespoons of the oil, the water, garlic, jalapeño, cilantro, mint, salt, ginger, mace, allspice, and remaining lemon juice. Pulse until it becomes a rough paste. Apply the spice paste to each side of the fish and inside of the cavity, making sure to get the paste into the gashes. Cover with plastic wrap and refrigerate for at least 4 hours, or up to overnight.

Preheat the oven to 400°F. Roast the fish for 15 minutes, flip the fish over, and roast for an additional 13 minutes. Turn the broiler to high. Broil the fish for 3 to 5 minutes, or until the herb paste sizzles on top. Serve with lemon wedges.

IF BOMBAY has a signature fish dish, then it must be whole pomfret cloaked in a multitude of spices called bottle masala. Every family in the state of Maharashtra (of which Bombay is the capital) has its own secret blend. This version of Bombay-style fish is a quick one, though it doesn't sacrifice flavor for speed. Intensely aromatic, the spice paste protects the fish from overcooking and seals in its juices.

spicy coconut and green chile stir-fried shrimp

SERVES 4 TO 6

2 pounds medium shrimp, peeled and deveined

1 teaspoon cayenne pepper

½ teaspoon turmeric

½ teaspoon powdered mustard

Juice of 1 lime plus extra lime wedges for serving

2 tablespoons canola oil

1 teaspoon black mustard seeds

20 fresh or frozen curry leaves, torn into pieces (optional)

1 red onion, thinly sliced

2 teaspoons kosher salt

3 tablespoons unsweetened shredded coconut

8 scallions, white and light green parts only, thinly sliced

2 to 4 jalapeños, finely chopped

Place the shrimp in a large bowl and sprinkle with the cayenne, turmeric, mustard powder, and lime juice. Stir to combine, cover with plastic wrap, and refrigerate for 30 minutes.

Heat the oil with the mustard seeds and curry leaves in a large skillet over medium-high heat until they start to crackle and the curry leaves turn crisp, 2 to 3 minutes. Add the red onion and the salt and cook, stirring often, for about 4 minutes or until they begin to brown. Add the coconut and cook until it starts to brown, 30 seconds. Stir in the shrimp and cook for 30 seconds to 1 minute, stirring often. Mix in the jalapeños and ¾ of the scallions and cook, stirring often, until the shrimp are curled and opaque, 1 to 3 minutes longer. Serve hot with the lime wedges and sprinkled with the remaining scallions.

THIS IS the kind of recipe that takes just minutes to make. It's delicious with or without the coconut, so feel free to omit it if you can't find any unsweetened shredded coconut in your local market.

chicken and turkey

In India, chicken is one of the most expensive proteins you can buy. Indians who eat meat give it a great place of pride in their kitchens and treat it as a highlight around which a meal is built. Chicken is embraced as a blank canvas, with marinades, spice pastes, and seasonings introduced to transform it into a celebration of spices and flavor.

Lean in fat and adaptable to almost any spice or sauce, chicken is accepted by most anyone at the dinner table. I approach cooking chicken and turkey as I do cooking vegetables and red meats. I marinate, I season, I add spice blends and seasoned oils, all with the aim of adding tenderness and deep flavor.

The Parmesan-Spiced Chicken Cutlets are simple, familiar, and accessible and yet will delight you with their unexpected hit of warm garam masala and crunchy panko bread-crumb coating. Marinated in sour cream, garlic, paprika, cardamom, and cumin, the Creamy Roast Chicken Breasts are easy and flavorful. This dish, called Malai Murgh in India, along with the Goat Cheese Pesto–Stuffed Chicken Breasts, challenges the notion that chicken breasts are bone dry and bland. For those who are partial to juicy dark meat, the Lemon Chicken Legs and Thighs may turn out to be one of your favorite recipes in this book. Fresh and citrusy, it has a great crispy skin to boot. It would also work beautifully with bone-in chicken breasts or even chicken wings.

Roasting a whole chicken is one of my favorite ways to prepare a juicy chicken with little to no effort. Butter and season the chicken, bake in the oven, and as it cooks, prepare a salad for a quick meal. While it roasts you can unwind and relax after a long and busy day and come to the table looking forward to the nourishing and healing meal ahead.

If you want to serve chicken for a party, try the Goat Cheese Pesto–Stuffed Chicken Breasts or the Fried Chicken Masala. The stuffed breasts have all the elegance you could ever wish for, while **the fried chicken is well suited to picnics and casual affairs—beautifully crispy and crusty, and as good as fried chicken gets.** This recipe is easy to double or triple for gatherings where you are called upon to feed battalions of people. Lastly, no repertoire could be complete without a roasted turkey. Brushed with tamarind glaze, this turkey brings a touch of exotica to the holiday table. If you are at a loss of ideas for what to do with the leftover turkey, try the recipe for Turkey Hash. It's excellent for breakfast or wrapped in a tortilla for a light dinner.

parmesan-spiced chicken cutlets

SERVES 4

½ cup fresh cilantro, finely chopped
6 garlic cloves, peeled and finely chopped
2 tablespoons extra-virgin olive oil
Juice of ½ lemon plus 1½ lemons, cut
   into wedges, for serving
1¼ teaspoons kosher salt
¾ teaspoon ground peppercorns
¼ teaspoon cayenne pepper
8 chicken breast cutlets

3 large eggs
¼ teaspoon Garam Masala (page 20)
1¾ cups panko bread crumbs
6 ounces Parmigiano-Reggiano cheese,
   finely grated (about 1¾ cups)
1 cup all-purpose flour
¼ to ½ cup extra-virgin olive oil or canola
   oil, for frying

Mix the cilantro, garlic, oil, lemon juice, 1 teaspoon of salt, ½ teaspoon of ground pepper-corns, and cayenne pepper in a small bowl. Transfer to a gallon-sized resealable plastic bag, add the chicken cutlets, and turn to coat. Refrigerate the cutlets for at least 30 minutes or overnight.

Whisk the eggs with the Garam Masala, ¼ teaspoon of salt, and ¼ teaspoon of ground peppercorns in a shallow dish. In a separate dish, stir together the bread crumbs and cheese. Place the flour in another dish. Dredge each chicken cutlet in the flour and tap off the excess. Dip into the egg mixture and then lay in the bread crumbs. Press the bread crumbs onto each side of the cutlets and place the breaded cutlets on a plate or baking sheet.

Heat a large skillet for 2 minutes over medium-high heat. Add the oil and heat for 1 to 2 min-utes or until very hot and shimmering. Fry the chicken in batches, cooking until both sides of the cutlets are golden brown, 3 to 4 minutes per side, adding extra oil to the skillet if and when necessary. Transfer the cutlets to a paper towel–lined plate to drain and serve with lemon wedges.

I LOOK TO THE INDIAN way of marinating meats to fortify the mild flavor of chicken cutlets. After resting in the cilantro-spiked marinade, they are dredged through flour, then spiced eggs, and finally coated with Parmigiano-Reggiano cheese and panko bread crumbs. This makes for a beautifully golden and crisp crust that provides depth of flavor from the very first bite.

goat cheese pesto–
stuffed chicken breasts

SERVES 8

FOR THE GOAT CHEESE PESTO

1½ cups pine nuts

2 loosely packed cups baby spinach

1 loosely packed cup basil leaves

4 ounces creamy chèvre-style goat cheese

½ cup golden raisins

1 tablespoon plus 1½ teaspoons extra-
   virgin olive oil

¾ teaspoon Garam Masala (page 20)

¼ teaspoon cayenne pepper

1 teaspoon kosher salt

¾ teaspoon ground peppercorns

FOR THE MARINADE

3 tablespoons chickpea flour (besan)

½ cup sour cream

2 garlic cloves, peeled and finely chopped

1 tablespoon extra-virgin olive oil

½ teaspoon kosher salt

½ teaspoon ground peppercorns

½ teaspoon turmeric

¼ teaspoon Garam Masala (page 20)

4 large boneless, skinless chicken breasts
   (about 7 to 8 ounces each), halved
   crosswise

Preheat the oven to 400°F. Make the pesto: Place the pine nuts on a rimmed baking sheet and toast until browned, 4 to 6 minutes, shaking the baking sheet midway through. Set aside to cool and then transfer to a food processor. Add the spinach, basil, goat cheese, raisins, oil, Garam Masala, cayenne pepper, salt, and ground peppercorns. Pulse until fairly smooth and set aside.

To make the marinade, heat the chickpea flour in a medium skillet over medium-high heat until it is browned, stirring often, 2 to 3 minutes (if the flour starts to get too dark, lift the skillet up off of the heat and stir to cool, then continue to toast over the flame). Transfer the toasted chickpea flour to a medium bowl and whisk in the remaining marinade ingredients.

Lay a long sheet of plastic wrap on your work surface. Place a chicken breast half in the center of the plastic wrap and fold one end of the plastic over it. Using the flat side of a meat mallet or the bottom of a heavy skillet, pound the chicken until it is ½ to ¼ inch thick. Remove the top sheet of plastic and add 1 to 3 tablespoons of pesto (the more you add, the richer the chicken will be) to the middle of the chicken. Use the plastic wrap to fold the chicken flaps over the filling and into a packet. Place it seam side down in a baking dish and repeat with the remaining chicken breast halves.

Spread the marinade over the chicken, making sure to get it all over and in between each rolled chicken breast. Cover the baking dish with plastic wrap and refrigerate for at least 30 minutes or overnight. Bake until the chicken is completely cooked through, 25 to 30 minutes, and serve.

ELEGANT AND FLAVORFUL, these stuffed chicken breasts are particularly well suited to dinner parties. The Mughals in India are believed to have often added dried fruits, like figs and apricots, to stuffings for meat. You can stuff the chicken breasts up to a day in advance. If you have pesto filling left over, save it to spread on crostini, toss with pasta, or just freeze for later.

lemon chicken legs and thighs

SERVES 4

4 chicken legs and thighs
2 tablespoons balsamic vinegar
2 lemons, zested, 1 juiced and the other
   cut into wedges
1 tablespoon plus 1 teaspoon kosher salt

2½ teaspoons ground peppercorns
2 tablespoons sugar
2 tablespoons canola oil
4 tablespoons unsalted butter,
   2 tablespoons cut into small pieces

Prick the chicken all over with a fork and set aside. Whisk the balsamic vinegar with half of the lemon zest, salt, and 2 teaspoons of ground peppercorns in a large bowl. Add the chicken and turn to coat. Refrigerate for 20 minutes or overnight. Mix the sugar with the remaining lemon zest and set aside.

Preheat the oven to 400°F. Heat the oil over medium-high heat in a large oven-safe skillet or braising dish until very hot, about 2 minutes. Add 2 tablespoons of the butter, and once melted, place the chicken, skin side down, in the skillet along with the remaining marinade. Cook until the chicken is browned on one side, 3 to 4 minutes, and then flip each piece and cook for 1 minute longer. Sprinkle some of the lemon sugar and ½ teaspoon of ground peppercorns over each piece of chicken and transfer the skillet to the oven. Roast the chicken until it is completely cooked through and a thermometer inserted into a thick part of the thigh reads 165°F, about 25 minutes. Remove the chicken from the oven and scatter the butter pieces and lemon juice over it. Serve once the butter is melted, with some of the pan sauce drizzled over the chicken and with lemon wedges on the side.

I USED TO MAKE this dish for my first roommate in New York City. He liked well-cooked chicken and challenged me to devise a way to keep it succulent and juicy. A quick marinade in balsamic vinegar with lots of lemon juice, a little sugar, and some butter was my solution.

fried chicken masala

SERVES 4

FOR THE BUTTERMILK BRINE
3 cups buttermilk
¼ cup kosher salt
2 tablespoons sugar
1½ teaspoons Garam Masala (page 20)
1 teaspoon ground coriander
1 teaspoon ground peppercorns
½ teaspoon ground ginger
½ teaspoon paprika
¼ teaspoon cayenne pepper

1 chicken (3½ to 4 pounds), cut into
    8 serving pieces
Canola oil, for frying
2 cups all-purpose flour
2 teaspoons ground coriander
2 teaspoons Garam Masala (page 20)
2 teaspoons ground peppercorns
1 teaspoon turmeric
½ teaspoon kosher salt
¼ teaspoon cayenne pepper

To make the brine, mix the buttermilk with all of the spices in a large bowl. Transfer to a gallon-sized resealable plastic bag. Add the chicken, turn to coat, and refrigerate overnight.

Heat 1 inch of canola oil in a large heavy-bottomed high-sided skillet over medium-high heat until it reaches 375°F. In a shallow bowl, whisk the flour with the spices and add the chicken pieces. Turn to coat in the flour and let the chicken rest in the flour until the oil gets hot. Tap off the excess flour and add as many pieces of chicken to the skillet as you can. Fry until browned, 6 to 8 minutes. Turn the chicken over and fry until the chicken is deeply browned on the other side, about another 6 to 8 minutes. Using tongs, transfer the chicken pieces to a paper towel–lined plate to drain. Serve while warm or at room temperature.

MY FRIENDS RENÉE and Carl Behnke are consummate hosts and gourmands, and fried chicken is one of their favorite dishes to offer a hungry crowd. Renée's secret for an amazingly crispy and crunchy crust, which is now mine (and yours), is to let the chicken rest in flour as the oil heats. I have adapted her recipe, giving it an Indian twist. Indians (like many southern Americans) love buttermilk, so it's natural to use it as a liquid for the overnight brine. I add spices to the brine and flour coating to give the chicken an extra hit of flavor.

spicy-sweet chicken wings

SERVES 4 TO 6

5 tablespoons honey

2 tablespoons canola oil

1 teaspoon kosher salt

1 teaspoon ground peppercorns

1 teaspoon Garam Masala (page 20)

1 teaspoon paprika

½ teaspoon cayenne pepper

½ teaspoon ground cumin

2 pounds chicken wings, halved at the drumette joint

1 tablespoon white wine vinegar

Coarse sea salt, for sprinkling

Preheat the oven to 400°F. Whisk 2 tablespoons of the honey with the oil, salt, ground peppercorns, Garam Masala, paprika, cayenne pepper, and cumin in a small bowl. Pour into a resealable gallon-sized plastic bag and add the chicken wings. Turn to coat with marinade and refrigerate for 30 minutes or up to overnight.

Line a baking sheet with aluminum foil and place a wire rack on top of the baking sheet (you can also line a broiler drip pan with foil and cut slits in the foil so the juices don't pool around the chicken). Arrange the chicken wings in a single layer on the rack. Roast for 35 minutes.

Whisk the remaining 3 tablespoons of honey and the vinegar in a small bowl. Remove the wings from the oven and brush with the honey-vinegar mixture. Continue roasting until the wings are slightly charred and crisp, another 15 to 25 minutes. Sprinkle with some coarse salt and cool for 5 minutes before serving.

CHICKEN WINGS have universal appeal, and people across cultures and continents find them delicious. Perhaps it is the crispiness of the skin, or the fact that people are open to making chicken wings spicy and intensely flavorful. These wings pack in spices, heat, and sweetness. Baking them instead of frying simplifies the cooking process, eliminating having to stand over a pot of hot oil. Feel free to add more cayenne pepper if you want super-hot wings. Double the recipe for a party-friendly yield.

creamy roast chicken breasts (malai murgh)

SERVES 4

Juice of ½ lemon
2 teaspoons kosher salt
1 teaspoon ground peppercorns
¼ teaspoon ground cardamom
¼ teaspoon paprika
⅛ teaspoon ground mace
4 garlic cloves, peeled

1 teaspoon cumin seeds
½ jalapeño (cored and seeded if you
  prefer a milder flavor)
4 boneless, skinless chicken breasts
  (6 to 8 ounces each)
¾ cup sour cream
2 tablespoons unsalted butter, melted

Whisk the lemon juice, salt, ground peppercorns, cardamom, paprika, and mace together in a small bowl. Using a mortar and pestle, grind the garlic, cumin seeds, and jalapeño into a rough paste. Add to the bowl with the spices and transfer to a gallon-sized resealable plastic bag. Add the chicken and turn to coat. Refrigerate for at least 20 minutes or up to overnight.

Add the sour cream to the chicken and turn the chicken to coat in the sauce. Preheat the oven to 500°F. Line a baking sheet with aluminum foil and place a wire rack on top of the baking sheet (you can also line a broiler drip pan with foil and cut slits in the foil so the juices don't pool around the chicken). Place the chicken on the rack, rounded side down, and roast for 15 minutes. Turn the breasts over and brush the tops with the melted butter. Roast until the chicken is completely cooked through and a digital thermometer inserted into the thickest part of the breast reads 160°F, another 15 to 20 minutes, and serve.

MY MOTHER ALWAYS took the time to grind spices with garlic and chiles using a mortar and pestle. She claimed that the essential oils that are released when you use a mortar and pestle make it worth the extra effort. When I have the time, I follow Mom's advice, but when I'm in a rush, I substitute ¾ teaspoon ground cumin and finely chop the garlic and jalapeño instead. Use the time while the chicken marinates and bakes to prepare a side dish like Coconut Rice (page 184) or a vegetable stir-fry.

lavender roast chicken

SERVES 4

FOR THE HERB RUB

3 garlic cloves, peeled and roughly chopped

1 tablespoon finely chopped fresh rosemary or thyme

1 teaspoon finely chopped fresh lavender

1¼ teaspoons paprika

1 tablespoon kosher salt

1 teaspoon ground peppercorns

6 tablespoons unsalted butter, at room temperature

1 chicken (3½ to 4 pounds), rinsed with cold water

10 fresh rosemary or thyme sprigs

5 fresh lavender sprigs

1 lemon, halved

1 tablespoon unsalted butter, melted

1 tablespoon balsamic vinegar

To make the herb rub, blend the garlic, chopped rosemary, lavender, paprika, salt, and ground peppercorns together using a mortar and pestle until it becomes a semismooth paste (or chop by hand or use a small food processor). Mix with the butter in a small bowl and set aside.

Preheat the oven to 400°F. Slide your fingers under the skin over the chicken breast, working your fingers down the meat to separate the skin from the meat and create a pocket. Continue to work your fingers down the chicken thighs and legs, creating a pocket between the thigh and leg meat and the skin. Stuff 2 tablespoons of herb butter under the skin of each breast, continuing to work it down under the skin of the thighs and legs. Massage the top of the chicken skin to work the butter into as even a layer as possible. Rub 1 tablespoon of butter all over the outside of the chicken and 1 tablespoon inside the chicken cavity. Stuff the rosemary sprigs, the lavender, and the lemon halves into the chicken cavity. Tie the chicken legs together with butchers' twine and tuck the wings under the breasts.

Place the chicken breast side down on a roasting rack set into a roasting pan. Roast for 30 minutes. Remove the chicken from the oven and brush it with ½ of the balsamic vinegar. Turn the chicken breast side up, brush with the remaining balsamic vinegar, and roast for an additional 15 minutes. Brush with the melted butter and roast until the chicken is cooked through, another 15 to 30 minutes, or until a digital thermometer inserted into the thick part of the thigh reads 165°F. Remove the chicken from the oven and let it rest for 10 minutes before carving and serving.

ULTRAFRESH HERBS and a farm-fresh chicken served as the inspiration for this French country-style Lavender Roast Chicken recipe. Feel free to add other savory herbs to the mix or use just one kind of fresh herb. If you don't have a mortar and pestle, you can finely chop all of the herb rub ingredients together, or use a small food processor or spice grinder to blend them.

tamarind-glazed turkey with corn bread–jalapeño stuffing

SERVES 10 TO 12

FOR THE TURKEY

4 cups kosher salt (or 2 cups table salt)

¼ cup dark brown sugar

1 teaspoon cayenne pepper

1 teaspoon ground coriander

1 teaspoon Toasted Cumin (page 16)

1 teaspoon Garam Masala (page 20)

1 teaspoon ground ginger

1 teaspoon ground peppercorns

1 teaspoon tamarind paste

6 quarts cold water

1 turkey (12 to 14 pounds), giblets, neck, and tailpiece removed, rinsed with cold water

1 tablespoon canola oil

FOR THE CORN BREAD STUFFING

1 recipe Grandma Hayes's Corn Bread (page 188), crumbled

2 cups fresh bread cubes

½ cup chicken or turkey broth

½ cup Tamarind Chutney (page 13), plus ¼ cup for serving

To prepare the turkey, whisk the salt, sugar, spices, and tamarind paste with 8 cups of warm water in a large bowl until dissolved. Pour into a large trash bag–lined cooler, or a large plastic tub. Add the cold water and whisk to incorporate. Add the turkey and submerge. Cover the pot or knot the bag to seal and refrigerate or place in a cold area (40°F or colder) for 8 hours or up to overnight.

Adjust an oven rack to the lowest position, and preheat the oven to 400°F. Grease a roasting rack with the canola oil and set into a heavy-bottomed roasting pan. Remove the turkey from the brine and pat dry with paper towels. Let the turkey rest at room temperature for 45 minutes; discard the brine.

To make the stuffing, combine the corn bread and the bread cubes in a large bowl. Drizzle the chicken or turkey broth around the sides of the bowl and toss to combine. Stuff the stuffing into the turkey's cavity. Tie the turkey legs together with butchers' twine and tuck the wings under the breasts. Brush the entire turkey with some Tamarind Chutney and place the turkey breast side down on the roasting rack.

Roast the turkey for 45 minutes, breast side down. Remove the roasting pan from the oven and, using two wadded-up bunches of paper towels, turn the turkey breast side up. Brush the breast with Tamarind Chutney and cover with a sheet of aluminum foil. Roast for another

45 minutes. Remove the roasting pan from the oven and remove the aluminum foil (reserve the foil for later). Brush the turkey with the remaining chutney. Return the turkey to the oven and roast for another 15 to 30 minutes, or until a digital thermometer inserted into the thick part of the thigh reads 165°F (if at any time the turkey looks like it is getting too dark, re-cover with aluminum foil). Remove the turkey from the oven and take the temperature of the stuffing. If the temperature is not at 160°F, then transfer the stuffing to a baking dish and bake for 10 to 15 minutes. Tent the turkey with the reserved foil and let it rest for 20 minutes. Carve and serve with stuffing and additional Tamarind Chutney on the side.

THANKSGIVING AND CHRISTMAS have become occasions for Charlie and me to open our home to friends and family visiting New York City for the holidays. We generally forgo the usual sit-down dinners, making the evening less formal with a food-packed buffet. This gives our guests the ability to chitchat and catch up, and gives us the time to cook up comforting and soulful dishes. This turkey blends comfort with just a hint of exotica, bringing all of our guests together where food, cultures, and heritage find a meeting point. Raquel, my coauthor, lines the vegetable bin of her fridge with a trash bag, then places the turkey and the brine in another trash bag and inserts it right into the vegetable bin. This keeps the turkey out of the way and maximizes precious refrigerator space.

day-after turkey hash masala

SERVES 6

6 large eggs
1 tablespoon kosher salt
½ teaspoon ground peppercorns
3 tablespoons canola oil
2 garlic cloves, peeled and finely minced
26 curry leaves, roughly torn (optional)
1 tablespoon cumin seeds
1 tablespoon black mustard seeds
4 dried red chiles

1 large red or yellow onion, halved and thinly sliced
1 jalapeño (cored and seeded if you prefer a milder flavor), chopped
4 cups shredded, cooked turkey or shredded deli turkey
2 large tomatoes, halved and thinly sliced
1 cup finely chopped fresh cilantro

Beat the eggs with 1 teaspoon of kosher salt and the ground peppercorns in a medium bowl and set aside.

Heat the oil with the garlic, curry leaves (if using), cumin seeds, mustard seeds, and chiles in a large skillet over medium-high heat until the cumin is fragrant and golden and the mustard seeds begin to pop, stirring often, for about 2 minutes. Add the onion, jalapeño, and 2 teaspoons of salt, and cook for 1 minute. Add the shredded turkey, cook for 1 minute, and then mix in the tomatoes. Reduce the heat to medium and cook until the tomatoes release their liquid, about 3 minutes, stirring occasionally.

Increase the heat to medium-high and pour in the eggs. Mix the eggs into the turkey and vegetables and cook until the eggs begin to set, stirring often, for 2 minutes. Mix in all but 2 tablespoons of the cilantro and cook for 30 seconds longer if you like soft eggs, or 1 minute longer if your prefer medium-cooked eggs. Transfer to a serving dish, sprinkle with the reserved cilantro, and serve.

A QUICK USE for leftover turkey, this meal can be prepared in less than 15 minutes and is great served with corn bread, over an English muffin or a bagel, or even wrapped in a tortilla. Gently sautéing the turkey with oil-toasted spices helps to seal in flavor and moisture, giving the turkey a pseudo-marinade effect. The addition of eggs not only binds the dish, but also provides for an underlying richness. If you don't have leftover turkey, it's excellent made with deli turkey or shredded rotisserie chicken.

pork, lamb, and beef

Though I grew up as an egg-and-milk-eating vegetarian, I now consider myself an occasional meat eater and I cook it often for guests.

Meat can deliver two very wonderful and yet different tastes. Pan-fried and broiled meats are simple and hearty. Roasted and braised meats are sultry and comforting. All pan-seared steaks or chops need is a spice rub, an herbed butter, or even just a sprinkle of salt and pepper to finish. Long, wet-cooked roasts are fall-apart tender and incredibly soothing with their deep and dramatic flavors. In this chapter you'll find recipes from both genres, some that take days to marinate and hours to cook (albeit unattendend), and others that take less than twenty minutes to get on the dinner table.

Few meats present as many opportunities for creativity as pork, with free-range pork having a taste and richness that cannot be matched by conventional pork. As a white meat, pork's advantage is that it can be substituted in most any chicken, lamb, or beef recipe. Cut a pork tenderloin into thick discs for a lighter version of Steak au Poivre with Cilantro-Garlic Butter or substitute pork cutlets for chicken in Parmesan-Spiced Chicken Cutlets.

Lamb can be cooked slowly, like the Tandoori-Spiced Leg of Lamb, or seared quickly as in the Lamb Loin Chops with Sambhaar. Since lamb is fatty, it is the perfect partner to robust and bold Indian spices and flavors. If you can source it and splurge on it, try cooking with grass-fed lamb. Its flavor is greater and more exciting on the tongue than grain-fed lamb, and its lively nuances stand up to strong seasoning. Jamison Farm in Pennsylvania has some of the best grass-fed lamb that you can find in the United States (for mail-order information, see page 253).

When shopping for steaks, I look for marbled meat that has been dry-aged for a couple of weeks. Dry-aging helps develop the flavor of beef and also tenderizes it, characteristics that are beneficial when cooking minimally, as you do steaks. If the meat has a dry sheen and is more purple than pink in color, you know it has been aged. While I use a filet for the Steak au Poivre in this chapter, feel free to substitute a more flavorful or bone-in cut, like a rib eye or New York strip steak (if using a thinner steak, you will want to reduce the time that the steak roasts in the oven). Post cooking, let the steak rest for a minute or two to reabsorb its juices—and take advantage of this time to add the finishing touches to side dishes.

pork chops with pear chutney

SERVES 4

2 tablespoons canola oil or extra-virgin
  olive oil
2 teaspoons ground coriander
1½ teaspoons ground peppercorns
1 teaspoon kosher salt

¼ teaspoon cayenne pepper
4 pork rib chops (8 ounces each),
  ¾ to 1 inch thick
½ recipe Spiced Pear Chutney (page 11)
1 teaspoon sugar

Place the oil, coriander, ground peppercorns, salt, and cayenne pepper in a gallon-sized reseal-able plastic bag. Add the pork chops and turn to coat. Refrigerate for 20 minutes, or up to overnight.

Set an oven rack in the upper-middle position and preheat the broiler. Heat a large oven-safe skillet for 2 minutes over medium-high heat. Add the pork chops (discard the marinade) and sear on one side until browned, about 3 minutes. Turn the chops over and transfer the skillet to the oven. Broil the chops for 3 minutes, remove the skillet from the oven, and spread 2 table-spoons of Pear Chutney evenly over each chop. Sprinkle each chop with ¼ teaspoon of sugar and return the skillet to the oven. Continue to broil the chops until the chutney is golden and even a little charred, 1 to 1½ minutes. Transfer the chops to a platter and serve with pan juices.

BECAUSE THERE IS OIL in the marinade, you can cook these chops in a skillet with no extra fat. If you don't have any Pear Chutney in the house, use applesauce spiked with a pinch of cayenne pepper.

honey-glazed pork roast with vegetable confit

SERVES 8

1 center-cut pork loin roast, trimmed

FOR THE SPICE PASTE
⅓ cup extra-virgin olive oil
3 tablespoons honey
2 tablespoons balsamic vinegar
2 tablespoons finely chopped fresh
thyme, or 1 tablespoon dried)
2 tablespoons finely chopped fresh
rosemary, or 1 tablespoon dried)
1 tablespoon ground peppercorns
1 tablespoon plus 1 teaspoon kosher salt
½ teaspoon red pepper flakes

FOR THE VEGETABLES
⅓ cup plus 1 tablespoon extra-virgin
olive oil
2 teaspoons balsamic vinegar
1 teaspoon finely chopped fresh thyme,
or ½ teaspoon dried
1 tablespoon plus 1 teaspoon kosher salt
2 teaspoons ground peppercorns
4 large red potatoes, coarsely chopped
2 large red onions, halved, thickly sliced,
and chopped crosswise
3 bell peppers, red and/or green, cored,
seeded, thickly sliced, and chopped
crosswise

Line a baking sheet with plastic wrap and place the pork roast on top. To make the spice paste, whisk all of the ingredients together in a medium bowl, then rub into the pork roast, taking care to get in between the bones and meat. Cover the roast with plastic wrap and marinate for at least 1 hour, or up to overnight.

Preheat the oven to 450°F and grease a sturdy roasting pan and roasting rack with 1 table-spoon of the olive oil. Prepare the vegetables: In a large bowl whisk together the remaining ⅓ cup of olive oil, balsamic vinegar, thyme, salt, and ground peppercorns. Add the chopped vegetables and toss to coat. Remove the roast from the refrigerator, place it on the greased rack, and roast it for 30 minutes. Reduce the oven temperature to 350°F and remove the roast-ing pan from the oven. Drain all but 1 tablespoon of fat from the roasting pan and add the veg-etables to the pan. Stir to coat with fat and place the roast fat side up over the vegetables. Roast for an additional 1¼ to 1½ hours, or until a meaty part of the roast reaches 155°F. Cover the roast with aluminum foil and let it rest for 15 minutes (the pork's internal temperature will increase to 160°F to 165°F). Carve and serve with the vegetables on the side.

THIS IS A HOLIDAY CENTERPIECE roast if there ever was one. I often prep the roast the day before and let it marinate overnight. With a built-in vegetable side dish, this recipe offers two dishes for the effort of one. It's amazing with Grandma Hayes's Corn Bread (page 188) and Spiced Pear Chutney (page 11).

tandoori-spiced leg of lamb

SERVES 8

FOR THE SOUR CREAM MARINADE

¾ cup sour cream

1 cup raw cashews

½ cup golden raisins

4 garlic cloves, peeled and roughly chopped

A 2-inch piece fresh ginger, peeled and roughly chopped

¼ cup lemon juice (from about 1 lemon)

2 tablespoons kosher salt

1½ teaspoons Garam Masala (page 20)

1 teaspoon ground peppercorns

¼ teaspoon cayenne pepper (optional)

¼ teaspoon ground cardamom

⅛ teaspoon ground mace

1 boneless leg of lamb (about 3½ pounds), tied into a roast

FOR THE SAUCE

¼ teaspoon saffron threads

6 cardamom pods, or ½ teaspoon ground cardamom

1½ cups whole milk

Blend all of the marinade ingredients in a food processor until smooth. Place the lamb on a cutting board and prick it all over with the tip of a paring knife. Place the lamb in a casserole or baking dish and cover with the marinade, spreading it all over and under the lamb and massaging it into the slits. Cover the casserole or baking dish with plastic wrap or a lid and refrigerate for 2 to 3 days.

Preheat the oven to 350°F. Remove the lamb from the refrigerator, uncover, and let it sit at room temperature for 30 minutes.

Place the saffron in a small skillet over medium-high heat and toast, while stirring, until the saffron is fragrant, 45 seconds to 1 minute. Transfer the saffron to a mortar and pestle (or, if using ground cardamom, to a small bowl) and grind with the seeds from the cardamom pods (if using ground cardamom, mash the saffron with the back of a spoon in a small bowl). Add 1 cup of the milk and stir to combine. Pour the saffron milk over the lamb and mix into the marinade, spooning it over the lamb.

Cover the casserole or baking dish with a lid or aluminum foil and bake for 2 hours. Reduce the oven temperature to 300°F and bake for an additional 30 minutes. Turn the oven off and let the lamb rest in the oven for 45 minutes. Remove the lamb from the oven and carefully transfer it to an aluminum foil–lined baking sheet. Remove the twine from the lamb. Stir the sauce in the casserole and spoon just enough over the lamb to make a thick coating.

Set an oven rack in the upper-middle position and heat your broiler to high. Broil the lamb for 5 minutes or until it is slightly charred and browned. Meanwhile, transfer the remaining sauce in the casserole dish to a medium saucepan. Whisk in the remaining $1/2$ cup of milk, bring to a boil, and turn off the heat. Transfer the broiled lamb to a serving platter and serve with extra sauce.

THIS RECIPE BORROWS from the extravagance of the Mogul period of Indian heritage. Of Mongol, Turkish, and Persian descent, these invaders came to India to take its riches, but found themselves in love with the land and its bountiful natural resources. This Tandoori-Spiced Leg of Lamb would have been an ideal centerpiece for a celebration centuries ago, just as it is today.

lamb loin chops with sambhaar

SERVES 4

8 lamb loin chops (about 4 pounds total)
3 tablespoons Sambhaar (page 21) or
    store-bought

2 teaspoons kosher salt
2 teaspoons canola oil or extra-virgin
    olive oil

Sprinkle both sides of the lamb chops with Sambhaar. Place them on a plate, cover with plastic wrap, and refrigerate for 20 minutes, or overnight.

Set an oven rack in the upper-middle position and heat your broiler to high. Remove the lamb chops from the refrigerator and sprinkle each side with a little salt. Heat a large skillet for 2 minutes over medium-high heat. Add the oil and the lamb chops and cook until they're browned on one side, 3 to 4 minutes. Drizzle a little oil over the chops and flip to the second side. Transfer the skillet to the oven and broil for 4 to 5 minutes (4 minutes for rare, 5 minutes for medium), or until they reach your preferred doneness. Remove the lamb chops from the oven, set aside for 5 minutes, and then serve.

LAMB LOIN CHOPS are the Rolls Royce of the lamb chop world. Because they're on the small side, I like to offer 2 chops per person. Sambhaar is a heady spice blend used often in southern India and it pairs nicely with lamb as well as steaks, chicken breasts, or pork chops, though you may have to adjust the cooking time to suit your preferred degree of doneness.

steak au poivre with cilantro-garlic butter

SERVES 6

FOR THE CILANTRO-GARLIC BUTTER
6 tablespoons (¾ stick) unsalted butter,
    at room temperature
½ cup fresh cilantro, roughly chopped
1 shallot, peeled and roughly chopped
2 garlic cloves, peeled and roughly
    chopped
1 lemon zested plus 2 tablespoons lemon
    juice (from about ½ lemon)

½ teaspoon Garam Masala (page 20)
½ teaspoon kosher salt

3 tablespoons ground peppercorns
    (preferably a mix of black, green, pink,
    and white peppercorns)
6 filet mignon steaks (6 to 8 ounces each)
Extra-virgin olive oil

To make the cilantro-garlic butter, pulse all of the ingredients together in a food processor, scraping the sides of the bowl as necessary, until the mixture is semismooth. Transfer the butter to a large piece of plastic wrap and pat into a log shape. Wrap plastic wrap around the butter and gently roll. Refrigerate for at least 1 hour or up to 3 days (you can also freeze the butter for up to 3 months).

Preheat the oven to 450°F. Place the ground peppercorns on your work surface and press the top and bottom of the filets into the pepper to coat the surface thickly. Heat an oven-safe skillet over medium-high heat for 2 minutes. Drizzle a little olive oil into the skillet and place the steaks in the skillet, searing until the peppercorns are browned on one side, about 3 minutes. Drizzle a little oil over the top of each steak and flip them over. Move the skillet to the oven and roast for 10 to 14 minutes (10 minutes for rare, 14 minutes for medium). Remove the skillet from the oven (remove the twine if your filets are tied) and transfer the steaks to individual plates. Slice the cilantro-garlic butter into six rounds and place one disc on top of each steak. Let the butter melt into the steak and then serve.

IT IS COMMON in Indian cooking to toast ground peppercorns in oil prior to adding other seasonings, vegetables, or meats. The oil coaxes out the heat of the peppercorn, allowing its flavor to permeate whatever else you add to the skillet. Mixed peppercorns contribute a complex flavor, but if you don't have any, then black peppercorns alone will do. You can follow the same procedure in this recipe with any other cut of beef, but take into consideration that bone-in and thinner steaks will cook faster than a thick, boneless steak.

indian-spiced meatballs with tomato-chile sauce

MAKES 3 DOZEN MEATBALLS

FOR THE SAUCE

¼ cup extra-virgin olive oil plus
   1 teaspoon, for greasing the baking dish
3 dried red chiles
½ teaspoon ground peppercorns
½ teaspoon chopped fresh rosemary, or
   ¼ teaspoon dried
½ teaspoon chopped fresh thyme,
   or ¼ teaspoon dried
1 large red onion, halved and thinly sliced
1 tablespoon kosher salt
2 red bell peppers, cored, seeded, and
   thinly sliced
1 tablespoon sugar
3 cups canned crushed tomatoes
1 cup water

FOR THE MEATBALLS

3 tablespoons extra-virgin olive oil
1 slice white or whole-wheat bread
¼ cup warm milk
1 pound ground beef (preferably 85% lean)
½ pound ground veal
1 large egg, lightly beaten
¼ cup fresh cilantro, finely chopped
3 garlic cloves, peeled and finely chopped
½ jalapeño (seeded and veined if you
   prefer a milder flavor), finely chopped
A 1-inch piece fresh ginger, peeled and
   grated
1 tablespoon kosher salt
1 teaspoon Garam Masala (page 20)
¼ teaspoon ground peppercorns
¼ teaspoon plus a pinch of cayenne
   pepper
2 tablespoons unsalted butter
½ cup slivered almonds

To make the sauce, heat the oil, chiles, and ground peppercorns in a large pot over medium-high heat, cooking until the pepper starts to sizzle, about 1½ minutes. Add the rosemary and thyme and cook until fragrant, 15 to 30 seconds. Add the onion and salt and cook until the onion is soft but not browned, stirring often, about 4 minutes. Reduce the heat to medium and add the bell peppers. Cook until they start to soften, stirring often, about 3 minutes. Mix in the sugar, reduce the heat to medium-low, cover the pot, and cook for 5 minutes, stirring halfway through. Add the tomatoes and bring to a boil, and then add the water and bring back to a boil. Reduce the heat to medium and partially cover the pot. Simmer for 20 minutes, stirring occasionally. Turn the heat off and set aside (at this point, the sauce can be refrigerated for up to 3 days or frozen for up to 3 months).

   Preheat the oven to 400°F. Grease a rimmed baking sheet with 1 tablespoon of olive oil and set it aside. Prepare the meatballs: Dip the bread in the warm milk and press it between your palms to squeeze out the excess liquid (discard leftover milk). Break the bread into small pieces and place in a large bowl. Add the beef, veal, remaining 2 tablespoons of olive oil, and egg and mix with your hands until the mixture is uniform in appearance and the bread is worked in. Add half of the cilantro, the garlic, jalapeño, ginger, salt, Garam Masala, ground peppercorns, and cayenne pepper and mix until it is completely integrated.

Melt the butter in a small skillet over medium heat. Add the almonds and a pinch of cayenne pepper, stirring and toasting the nuts until they are light brown and fragrant, 1 to 1½ minutes. Add the remaining cilantro and cook for an additional 30 seconds. Transfer the almonds to a spice grinder or mortar and pestle and grind into a coarse paste.

Form the meat mixture into small balls about the size of a Ping-Pong ball. Take one in your palm and make an indentation in the center with your finger. Add ¼ teaspoon of the almond spice paste and pinch the meatball shut so the spice mix is completely enclosed. Re-form the meat into a ball. Place the filled meatballs on a baking sheet and bake until firm and browned, 18 to 20 minutes, gently rolling after 10 minutes and then again after 5 minutes so they brown evenly. Toss with the tomato sauce and serve.

I'VE BORROWED the premise behind Lamb Seekh Kebabs (page 204), made with ground lamb, cilantro, chiles, and spices, for these mini-meatballs. They are made into small polpettini-style meatballs so you can easily add them to a recipe, like Spinach Lasagna with Roasted Eggplant Sauce (page 98) or the Baked Ziti with Vegetable Sauce (page 92). Or serve them as a fun passed hors d'oeuvres with tomato sauce on the side.

tamarind-glazed meat loaf

MAKES 2 LOAVES, EACH SERVING 4 TO 6

FOR THE MEAT LOAF

3 tablespoons unsalted butter

1/2 cup fresh bread crumbs

1/2 cup water

3 tablespoons canola oil

1 large red onion, thinly sliced

2 teaspoons kosher salt

A 1-inch piece fresh ginger, peeled and finely minced

4 garlic cloves, peeled and finely minced

1/2 jalapeño pepper (cored and seeded for a milder flavor), finely minced

2 teaspoons ground coriander

1 teaspoon ground cumin

1 teaspoon ground peppercorns

4 portobello mushroom caps (about 1 pound), finely diced

1/2 teaspoon cayenne pepper

1 teaspoon Garam Masala (page 20)

2 1/2 pounds ground beef (preferably 80% lean)

1 1/4 pounds ground pork

1 red bell pepper, cored, seeded, and finely chopped

1/4 cup fresh cilantro, finely chopped

3 large eggs

1/2 cup ketchup

2 ounces Parmigiano-Reggiano cheese, grated

1/2 teaspoon sweet paprika

FOR THE TAMARIND GLAZE

1 cup ketchup

1 teaspoon tamarind paste

2 teaspoons ground coriander

1 teaspoon ground cumin

1 teaspoon ground peppercorns

1/2 teaspoon cayenne pepper

To prepare the meat loaf, melt the butter in a medium skillet over medium-high heat. Add the bread crumbs and toast until browned, stirring often, for 3 to 5 minutes. Transfer to a large bowl and set aside to cool.

Place the water next to your cooktop. Heat the oil with the onion and salt in a large pot over medium-high heat, cooking the onion until it's soft and just starting to brown, stirring often, 4 to 5 minutes. Stir in the ginger and cook, stirring often to prevent the ginger from burning, and splashing with water if it starts to brown too much, until it's fragrant, about 30 seconds. Add the garlic and jalapeño and cook until the garlic is fragrant, splashing with water if necessary, for about 1 minute. Stir in the coriander, cumin, and ground peppercorns and cook for 1 minute, stirring and scraping the bottom of the skillet often and splashing it with water whenever the spices or onion begin to stick to the bottom of the pan.

Add the mushrooms and cook, stirring often, until they release their liquid and the liquid has evaporated, 6 to 8 minutes. Stir in the cayenne pepper and cook for 30 seconds. Stir in the Garam Masala, turn off the heat, and set the pot aside to cool.

Preheat the oven to 300°F. Add the remaining ingredients to the bowl with the toasted bread crumbs, kneading it until everything is completely incorporated. Add the cooled mushroom mixture and knead again until combined. Divide the mixture evenly into two 8$\frac{1}{2}$ x 4$\frac{1}{2}$-inch loaf pans and bake for 1 hour (or cover the loaf pan with plastic wrap, place inside of a resealable freezer bag, and freeze for up to 3 months; defrost overnight in your refrigerator before baking).

While the meat loaves bake, make the tamarind glaze. In a small bowl whisk the glaze ingredients together. Remove the loaves from the oven and carefully drain off the pooled fat from the pan. Evenly spread some glaze over each meat loaf and continue to bake for an additional 30 minutes, or until the internal temperature reads 165°F on a digital thermometer. Let the loaves cool for 15 minutes before serving. Run a knife around the pan's edges, slice, and serve.

RICHARD ARAKELIAN, the national chef for Sodexho and a good friend, was kind enough to share his famous meat loaf recipe with me. Rich's Armenian heritage, his savvy as a father who needs to feed his kids wholesome food, and his own love of and belief in eating healthfully and heartily all contributed to this clever recipe. Mushrooms contribute a nice moisture and the spices add an unexpected earthy undertone. This is excellent with the Roasted Baby Potatoes with Southern Indian Spices (page 177). This recipe makes enough for two loaves. Bake them both, or freeze one for another time.

CHAPTER 9

vegetables and side dishes

Abha Aunty's Sweet-and-Sour Eggplant

Brussels Sprouts with Apples and Almonds

Cardamom-Roasted Cauliflower

Stir-Fried Cabbage with Red Peppers and Peas

Cheesy Scalloped Corn

Green Beans with Coconut

Green Peas in Spiced Cream Sauce

Balsamic-and-Honey-Glazed Onions

Mashed Potatoes with Mustard Oil, Cilantro, and Onions

Roasted Baby Potatoes with Southern Indian Spices

Sweet Potato Chaat

Not-So-Dull Dal

Cumin-and-Cardamom-Scented Basmati Rice

Coconut Rice

Tamarind Rice

Pearl Couscous with Tomatoes

Grandma Hayes's Corn Bread

It is said that no one makes vegetarian food as well as we do in India, where vegetables are romanced and entertained in ways never imagined elsewhere. I choose to be more generous with accolades for vegetable dishes; Italians, Mexicans, Israelis, Arabs, South East Asians, and many Mediterranean countries have a great tradition of celebrating vegetables in ways not too dissimilar from Indians.

Though my background in cooking is distinctly Indian, I have freely borrowed techniques and flavors from these other cultures; I am a true American in this respect. From using honey in my glazes for roasted vegetables to my risotto-style approach in making couscous, I combine seasonings, spices, and approaches to come up with vegetable and side dishes that are healthy, often easy, and always tasty.

When my father became ill a few years ago, my whole family spent several months in Denver, where he was in the hospital. During this time, I took a remedial class in cooking from Mom, relearning how to make all of Dad's favorite foods. She taught me to keep everything delicious and simple. I like to think that dishes like Stir-Fried Cabbage with Red Peppers and Peas, his absolute favorite, prepared with flavors from home like fresh ginger, dried red chiles, and fenugreek leaves, helped to nurse him back to health. Recipes so easy to make, like dal and rice and cabbage, brought comfort to my family as we gathered around the table to replenish our energy after a long day at the hospital.

Few people are immune to the appeal of these vegetable dishes. By adding an unusual ingredient or two, like aged Gouda in the corn or coconut in the green beans (not unusual for Indians, but indeed strange to Americans!), these vegetables, which are already a part of your repertoire, can take on new life.

Seasoning humble vegetables and grains is how Indians take the most modest and inexpensive ingredients and turn them into food we crave. In India, we always flavor our food with lots of herbs, spices, and roots. By gently frying cumin and chiles in oil, making spice pastes with fresh ginger and cilantro, freshly grinding coriander, and making our own spice blends like Sambhaar and Garam Masala, it's possible to turn common vegetables like peas and butternut squash into dishes to get excited about.

There are lots of shortcuts to explore when cooking with vegetables. There is no way to measure how much time I have saved by using the precut vegetables sold at the supermarket, like freshly shelled peas, cubed butternut squash, and cauliflower florets. Though I never use canned vegetables (save for canned tomatoes that don't contain any preservatives or flavorings), I sometimes use frozen vegetables like green peas, corn, spinach, and French-cut green beans. There is no shame in being a savvy, practical cook, especially if it encourages you to cook and eat vegetables more often.

While certainly not a tome on the cookery of vegetables, this chapter offers enough variety of technique and spicing so that once you're comfortable with the recipes here, you may find yourself a pro at getting exciting vegetables, starches, and legumes on the table. In a world where we're constantly told to eat more vegetables, fruits, nuts, and grains, we need to remember that it helps for vegetables and grains to be cooked with care so eating them doesn't become a chore.

abha aunty's sweet-and-sour eggplant

SERVES 8

FOR THE EGGPLANT

1½ pounds round baby eggplants, ends trimmed, or 2 to 3 long Japanese eggplants, cut in 1½-inch-thick rounds

1 teaspoon kosher salt

¼ teaspoon cayenne pepper

Canola oil, for frying

FOR THE SAUCE

3 tablespoons canola oil

1½ teaspoons mustard seeds

1 teaspoon cumin seeds

16 curry leaves, roughly torn

4 dried red chiles

1 medium red onion, finely chopped

1 tablespoon plus 1 teaspoon kosher salt

2 teaspoons ground coriander

2 teaspoons ground cumin

¼ teaspoon cayenne pepper

2 medium tomatoes, finely chopped

1 cup canned chopped tomatoes

¼ cup Tamarind Chutney (page 13)

¼ cup water

To prepare the eggplant, use a paring knife to cut an X into the bottom (or end) of each eggplant. Mix the kosher salt with the cayenne pepper. Squeeze the eggplants to open the incision and sprinkle a little seasoned salt inside of the eggplant. Set aside in a bowl for 15 minutes.

Heat enough canola oil to fill a large saucepan by 2 inches to 350°F. Add just a few eggplants to the pan, reduce heat to medium, and fry until the eggplant is golden brown and slightly soft, 4 to 5 minutes. Transfer the fried eggplant to a paper towel–lined plate. Bring the oil back to 350°F before frying remaining batches of eggplant.

In a large saucepan, heat the 3 tablespoons of canola oil with the mustard seeds, cumin seeds, curry leaves, and chiles over medium-high heat, stirring often and cooking until the cumin is browned and the mustard seeds start to pop, 2½ to 3 minutes. Add the onion and salt and cook, stirring often, until the onion turns golden and becomes crispy, 6 to 8 minutes. Add the ground coriander, cumin, and cayenne pepper and cook for 1 minute, then add the fresh tomatoes, cooking until they begin to break down and get jammy, about 2 minutes. Stir in the canned tomatoes, cook 1 minute, and then add the chutney, and cook for an additional 30 seconds. Add the fried eggplant and water and bring to a simmer. Reduce the heat to medium-low, cover, and cook for 3 minutes. Remove the cover, increase the heat to high, and cook until the sauce reduces slightly and begins to stick to the bottom of the pan, 1 to 2 minutes. Taste for seasoning and serve.

ABHA AUNTY is one of my mother's best friends and was a neighbor when I was growing up. Now that I am a chef, whenever I visit she makes a few dishes to show off her repertoire. This dish is my favorite and has become quite a hit at my New York City restaurant. Cutting an X in the bottom of the eggplant allows it to cook more quickly and also gets the flavor of the sauce into the center of the eggplant.

brussels sprouts with apples and almonds

SERVES 8

3 pounds Brussels sprouts, ends trimmed and outer leaves removed

1 tablespoon balsamic vinegar

3 Granny Smith apples, cored and thinly sliced

1 cup sliced almonds

1 tablespoon kosher salt

1 teaspoon ground peppercorns

4 tablespoons canola oil or extra-virgin olive oil

2 small red onions, thinly sliced

1/3 cup raisins or currants

1/2 teaspoon red pepper flakes

1/2 cup (1 stick) unsalted butter, cut into small pieces

Set one oven rack to the center position and one to the upper-middle position. Preheat the oven to 350°F. With a paring knife, cut an X into the bottom of each of the Brussels sprouts and then place them in a large bowl. Add the vinegar, apples, almonds, salt, ground peppercorns, oil, onions, raisins, and pepper flakes. Toss together and transfer to a gratin or baking dish. Dot the top with half of the butter.

Bake the Brussels sprouts on the lower rack for 30 minutes. Sprinkle the remaining butter over the top and bake for another 30 minutes. Turn on the broiler. Place the baking dish on the upper-middle rack and broil for 2 minutes, or until the top layer of the casserole is browned (watch carefully as broiler intensity varies). Taste for seasoning and serve.

THIS IS THE ONLY WAY that I will eat Brussels sprouts. I learned this recipe from two talented Philadelphia-based artists and good friends, Daniel Heyman and Vincent Renou, who made it for me when they came to visit. It was the first time I had ever had Brussels sprouts that I actually liked, and I couldn't believe how delicious they were. Now, whenever I see beautiful Brussels sprouts at the greenmarket or grocery store, this is how I prepare them, especially for the holidays.

cardamom-roasted cauliflower

SERVES 8

⅓ cup extra-virgin olive oil plus extra,
    for greasing baking dish
3 green cardamom pods
3 dried red chiles (optional)
1 tablespoon coriander seeds
1 teaspoon cumin seeds

½ teaspoon whole peppercorns
1 head of cauliflower (2½ to 3 pounds),
    cored and broken into medium florets
1 medium red onion, halved and thinly
    sliced
Kosher salt, for sprinkling

Preheat the oven to 425°F. Grease a 9 x 13-inch baking dish or large gratin dish with olive oil and set aside.

Grind the cardamom pods, chiles, coriander, cumin, and whole peppercorns in a coffee grinder or small food processor until fine. Mix the spices with the oil in a large bowl. Add the cauliflower and onion and toss to coat. Transfer the vegetables to a baking dish and roast until they're tender, about 1 hour, stirring every 20 minutes. Sprinkle with salt and serve.

COARSE KOSHER SALT, or even Maldon sea salt, adds a lovely crunch to this otherwise ultratender roasted cauliflower.

stir-fried cabbage with red peppers and peas

SERVES 6

3 tablespoons canola oil
1½ teaspoons cumin seeds
1 teaspoon turmeric
3 dried red chiles
1 head of cabbage (about 3½ pounds), cored and finely chopped

2 red bell peppers, cored, seeded, and finely chopped
1 cup frozen peas
1½ teaspoons kosher salt

Heat the canola oil with the cumin seeds, turmeric, and chiles in a large pot or wok over medium-high heat, stirring occasionally, until the chiles become smoky, about 3 minutes. Add half of the cabbage and all of the bell peppers and frozen peas and stir to combine with the spices. After a couple of minutes the cabbage will start to wilt. Now stir in the remaining cabbage. Cook, stirring often, until the volume has reduced by a third and the cabbage looks very browned, 15 to 30 minutes (depending on your pot or wok). Mix in the salt and serve warm or at room temperature.

AS A CHILD, I didn't care for cabbage and could only eat it if it was al dente. Dad preferred it soft and browned. Now I find myself craving it his way, finding solace in its earthy brownness. This is a recipe that my friend Alice Fixx would always bring her Tupperware for. After dinner, I happily sent her home with the leftovers. She said it reminded her of her eastern European heritage. The key to caramelizing the cabbage is to wait until the end of the cooking process to salt it—otherwise, too much water will be released, inhibiting caramelization. With this cabbage, some dal, and rice, I am completely satisfied.

cheesy scalloped corn

SERVES 8 TO 10

6 ears of corn, husked
1 cup heavy cream
½ cup milk
5 tablespoons unsalted butter
1 jalapeño (cored and seeded if you prefer a milder flavor), finely chopped (optional)
¾ teaspoon ground peppercorns

¼ teaspoon red pepper flakes (optional)
2 tablespoons all-purpose flour
2 large eggs
⅔ pound aged Gouda, grated
½ teaspoon kosher salt
¾ cup dry bread crumbs or panko bread crumbs

Preheat the oven to 400°F. Place a box grater in a large, wide bowl and grate 3 ears of corn on the large-hole side, making sure that all of the corn's juices go into the bowl. Slice away the kernels from the remaining 3 ears and add them to the bowl with the corn milk. Mix the cream and milk in a measuring cup and set aside.

Place 2 tablespoons of butter in a large saucepan along with the jalapeños (if using), ½ teaspoon of the ground peppercorns, and pepper flakes (if using) and cook over medium-high heat until the butter is melted and the jalapeño is slightly soft, about 1½ minutes. Reduce the heat to medium, whisk in the flour, and cook for another minute. Drizzle in a couple of tablespoons of milk and whisk in. Repeat, whisking in a few tablespoons of milk at a time, until the flour paste is somewhat loose, and then add the remaining milk, whisking until smooth. Turn off the heat and whisk in the eggs. Stir in 1 cup of grated cheese and the salt, stirring until the cheese is melted. Pour the sauce over the corn.

Combine the remaining cheese with ¼ cup of the bread crumbs and the remaining ¼ teaspoon of cracked peppercorns in a small bowl and set aside. Melt 3 tablespoons of butter in a medium skillet over medium-high heat. Add the remaining ½ cup of bread crumbs and toast until deep brown, 2 to 5 minutes, stirring often so they don't burn. Stir the toasted bread crumbs into the corn mixture and transfer it to a large gratin or casserole dish. Top with an even layer of the bread crumb–cheese mixture and bake until it is browned and a toothpick inserted into the center comes out clean, about 30 minutes. Serve hot.

MY PARTNER CHARLIE, who grew up in West Virginia, always used to brag about the amazing scalloped corn from his hometown. In an effort to prepare something special for him, I decided to cobble together this recipe, using fresh corn and aged Gouda, adding some chopped jalapeño and red pepper flakes to give it an Indian edge. Grating corn on a box grater extracts the sweet and vibrantly yellow corn milk. It is the "secret ingredient" to my scalloped corn that will make any Southerner proud.

green beans with coconut

(green bean poriyal)

SERVES 6

¼ cup canola oil
1 tablespoon mustard seeds
24 curry leaves, roughly torn (optional)
1¼ teaspoons cumin seeds
¾ cup unsweetened shredded coconut

1 pound green beans, cut into bite-sized
  pieces
1½ teaspoons kosher salt
1 cup water

Combine the oil and the mustard seeds in a large skillet or wok. Cook over medium-high heat until the mustard seeds start to pop, $1^1/_2$ to 2 minutes. Add the curry leaves and cumin seeds and cook, stirring often, until the cumin becomes fragrant and browned, $1^1/_2$ to 2 minutes. Add $^1/_4$ cup of the coconut and cook until it turns a toasty brown color, 15 to 30 seconds, stirring continuously so the coconut doesn't burn.

Add the green beans and the salt and cook for 5 minutes, stirring occasionally. Add the remaining $^1/_2$ cup of coconut and the water and bring to a simmer. Cover the skillet and reduce the heat to medium-low. Cook until the green beans are tender, about 10 minutes. Uncover, increase the heat to medium, and cook until all of the water is evaporated, stirring often, 5 to 8 minutes. Taste for seasoning and serve.

THOUGH THIS IS POPULAR in southern Indian vegetarian homes, it's the kind of delicious, full-flavored dish that even nonvegetarian Southerners relish. One of its charms is how simple it is to make. You can substitute any bite-sized vegetable for the green beans—try it with zucchini or cabbage, two of my favorites. While coconut, mustard seeds, and curry leaves are a constant trio, other spices can be eliminated or added as you please. If using frozen green beans, use half as much water at the end of the recipe.

green peas in a spiced cream sauce
(doodh walee matar)

SERVES 4

3 tablespoons canola oil
2 teaspoons ground coriander
½ teaspoon cumin seeds
½ teaspoon turmeric
⅛ teaspoon cayenne pepper

⅛ teaspoon asafetida (optional)
2½ cups frozen petite peas
1 cup whole milk
1 teaspoon kosher salt

Heat the oil with the coriander, cumin seeds, turmeric, cayenne pepper, and asafetida (if using) in a large saucepan over medium-high heat, cooking until the cumin turns light brown and fragrant, 1½ to 2 minutes. Mix in the frozen peas and reduce the heat to low. Cook, covered, until the peas are soft and the moisture is evaporated, stirring often, for about 5 minutes.

Stir in the milk and salt. Bring to a simmer and then reduce the heat to low. Cover the pan and cook for 5 more minutes. Remove the cover, increase the heat to medium, and continue cooking, stirring occasionally, until the sauce is thick enough to coat the back of a spoon, 6 to 8 minutes longer. Taste for seasoning and serve.

I MAKE THIS for Jain friends, whose religion doesn't permit them to eat any root vegetables, including onions and garlic. Asafetida, which traditionally stands in for those vegetables, gives the sauce a savory, garlicky taste. The milk makes it creamy without being too rich. This tastes excellent with pooris, plain basmati rice, or warmed pita bread.

balsamic-and-honey-glazed onions

SERVES 8

½ cup extra-virgin olive oil plus extra, for
greasing the baking dish
¼ cup balsamic vinegar
⅔ cup honey
1½ teaspoons chopped fresh rosemary

1½ teaspoons chopped fresh thyme
leaves
1 teaspoon kosher salt
½ teaspoon ground peppercorns
10 small red onions (about 3 pounds),
root end trimmed and halved

Preheat the oven to 400°F. Grease a large baking dish with oil and set aside. Whisk the oil, balsamic vinegar, honey, rosemary, thyme, salt, and ground peppercorns together in a large bowl. Add the onions and toss with the glaze. Transfer to a baking dish and roast until the glaze is thick and bubbling, turning and basting the onions every 30 minutes, for 1½ to 2 hours. Cool for 30 minutes and serve while still warm or at room temperature.

THESE ONIONS are a staple on my dinner table. They are amazing with meats—Creamy Roast Chicken Breasts (page 140) and Pork Chops with Pear Chutney (page 149)—as well as with any vegetarian biriyani or side dish. Just toss them together in the morning, roast them, and leave them out at room temperature until you're ready to serve. Make a double batch—one for now, one for tomorrow; they're heavenly with eggs for breakfast or on an antipasto platter. Don't use up your good balsamic here; the cheap supermarket stuff works beautifully. You can also make this with red peppers or a combination of vegetables, like fennel, carrots, and onions.

mashed potatoes with mustard oil, cilantro, and onions (aloo bharta)

SERVES 8

1 medium red onion, quartered and thinly
   sliced
Juice of ½ lemon
6 medium (about 2 pounds) red potatoes
1 cup chopped fresh cilantro

1 jalapeño (cored and seeded if you prefer
   a milder flavor), finely chopped
1 tablespoon mustard oil
1½ teaspoons kosher salt

Place the onion in a large bowl. Mix with the lemon juice and set aside.

Place the potatoes in a large pot, cover with water, and bring to a boil, cooking them until they're tender. Drain and set aside. When cool enough to handle, peel the potatoes and set them aside to come to room temperature.

Add the cilantro and jalapeño to the onions. Add the mustard oil, salt, and potatoes. Mash the potatoes with the other ingredients, stirring, mashing, and pressing against the bottom and sides of the bowl until the mixture is creamy with some chunks. Serve immediately or leave at room temperature and serve within 6 hours. Though you can refrigerate it, this dish will lose some of its pungency if eaten the next day.

MARINA AHMED ALAM, my music teacher and one of the most revered exponents of classical Hindustani music, first made me this dish. Originally from Bangladesh, she now lives in New York City, where she teaches music, and even after a long day of work, will cook the most delightful meals. In my New York restaurant, our Bengali chefs often know to make this dish for me when I'm in a sour mood—it always makes me smile. Dense and a little chunky, these mashed potatoes are made without butter or dairy. The mustard oil and raw red onions make it very pungent and divine when served alongside modestly spiced foods. While it's good warm, it's also excellent served at room temperature (it almost tastes like potato salad). If you can't find mustard oil, you can use lemon juice and some olive oil instead, though it won't have the same sharpness.

roasted baby potatoes with southern indian spices

SERVES 8

¼ cup canola oil plus extra, for greasing baking dish

3 pounds baby red potatoes, rinsed and halved (larger potatoes quartered)

20 curry leaves (optional)

6 dried red chiles

2 teaspoons mustard seeds

1½ teaspoons cumin seeds

A 1-inch piece fresh ginger, peeled and finely minced

3 garlic cloves, peeled and finely minced

½ jalapeño (cored and seeded if you prefer a milder flavor), finely chopped

1 teaspoon turmeric

1 tablespoon kosher salt

½ cup chopped fresh cilantro

½ cup chopped fresh mint leaves

1 lime, half juiced and the other half cut into wedges for serving

¼ teaspoon cayenne pepper

Preheat the oven to 400°F. Grease a large, deep baking dish with some oil, add the potatoes, and set aside.

Heat the oil with the curry leaves (if using), chiles, mustard seeds, and cumin seeds in a large skillet until the mustard seeds start to crackle and pop, about 1½ minutes. Stir in the ginger, garlic, and jalapeño and cook, stirring often, until the garlic is fragrant, about 1 minute. Add the turmeric and salt and cook for 1 minute. Pour the spices over the potatoes and stir until evenly coated.

Bake the potatoes until tender and browned, 25 to 40 minutes, stirring every 10 minutes. Remove the baking dish from the oven and stir in the cilantro, mint, lime juice, and cayenne pepper. Serve with lime wedges.

THOUSANDS OF YEARS AGO, garlic was considered an aphrodisiac and wasn't used in cooking—even today, observant Vaishnav Hindus don't use garlic. Indian cuisine essentially evolved without the addition of garlic in many of its recipes and the Indian palate became accustomed to a garlic-free diet. This is one of the few dishes in Indian vegetarian cooking in which garlic is used. It comes from the state Andhra Pradesh in the southern India planes, where people love to eat garlic.

sweet potato chaat

SERVES 6 TO 8

2½ pounds (about 5 medium) sweet
   potatoes
4 cups canola oil
1 to 2 tablespoons kosher salt

1 to 2 tablespoons Toasted Cumin
   (page 16)
1 to 2 tablespoons chaat masala
⅛ to ¼ teaspoon cayenne pepper
2 limes, cut into wedges

Preheat the oven to 450°F. Prick the sweet potatoes with a fork and then place them on an aluminum foil–lined baking sheet. Bake until the skins are baggy and the flesh gives to slight pressure, about 1 hour (less for small sweet potatoes and longer for large ones). Set the potatoes aside to cool completely and then peel and chop them into cubes. Reduce the oven temperature to 350°F.

Heat the canola oil in a large pot or wok until it registers between 325°F and 350°F on a thermometer. Using a slotted spoon, add about ¼ of the potato cubes (take care not to overcrowd the pot because the oil will cool) and fry, stirring, turning, and breaking the potatoes apart if they stick together. Fry until they are blistered and browned, 4 to 6 minutes. Transfer them to a paper towel–lined plate and set them aside or keep them warm on a baking sheet in the hot oven. Let the oil return to 325°F to 350°F before frying the remaining batches of potatoes.

Once all of the potatoes are fried, transfer them to a bowl and toss with a few pinches of kosher salt, Toasted Cumin, chaat masala, cayenne to taste, and some fresh lime juice. Taste and adjust with additional spices or lime juice as you like. Serve while hot or at room temperature.

I RECALL THE AMAZING char-grilled smell of shakar kandi, Sweet Potato Chaat, almost as fondly as I recall its flavor. As a child, I remember how vendors would approach my gate pushing their rustic Old World wooden carts outfitted with big griddles and fueled by burning coals, ready to provide my brother, sister, and me with this most delicious after-school snack. The sweet potatoes were cooked until sugary and tender over hot coals and then cut into cubes, fried, and tossed with spices like chaat masala, lime juice, cumin, and salt—sweet, sour, salty, and savory. Though traditionally a street food, these potatoes make a welcome, exotic addition to any holiday or autumn table. Or for fun, serve as a passed hors d'oeuvres in little paper cones.

not-so-dull dal

SERVES 6

3 tablespoons canola oil

2 teaspoons cumin seeds

3 dried red chiles

Pinch asafetida (optional)

1 medium red onion, halved and thinly sliced

1 jalapeño (cored and seeded if you prefer a milder flavor), finely chopped

1 tablespoon kosher salt

2 garlic cloves, peeled and finely chopped

1½ cups washed masoor dal or yellow split peas (channa dal)

6 cups water

Juice of ½ lemon

Heat the oil with cumin and chiles in a medium saucepan over medium-high heat for 1½ minutes. Add the asafetida (if using) and cook for 20 seconds and then add the onion and jalapeño. Cook for 1 minute, stir in the kosher salt, and cook until the onion and jalapeño have softened, about 3 minutes, stirring often. Add the garlic and lentils and cook until garlic becomes fragrant, 1 to 1½ minutes. Stir in ¼ cup of the water, cook until the pan is dry, and then add an additional 5¾ cups water and the lemon juice. Bring to a boil and then reduce heat to a simmer. Partially cover and stir every 10 minutes until the lentils are soft and break apart easily, but aren't completely broken down, 25 to 35 minutes. Taste for seasoning and serve with rice.

DAL IS MY EQUIVALENT of chicken soup. It's what I eat when I need something comforting, something to remind me of my kitchen in India. I like my dal with texture, but some people prefer it completely smooth. For a satiny smooth rendition, add a little water once the lentils have finished cooking and whisk vigorously. If you have fresh curry leaves in the house, add about 12 of them, along with 1 teaspoon of mustard seeds, to the oil and spices in the very beginning. The curry leaves and mustard seeds give the dal depth and spice. If you want to make a heartier dal, substitute 2 chopped tomatoes for the lemon juice and add them with the last addition of water. This is great with simple basmati rice and pita or parathas.

cumin-and-cardamom-scented basmati rice

SERVES 8

3 tablespoons canola oil
6 green cardamom pods
6 whole cloves
2 teaspoons cumin seeds

1 teaspoon coriander seeds
2 cups basmati rice
4 cups water

Heat the oil with the spices in a medium and wide saucepan until they're fragrant and the cumin is browned, $1^{1}/_{2}$ to 2 minutes, stirring occasionally. Add the rice and stir occasionally, cooking for 2 minutes. Add the water and bring it to a boil. Reduce the heat to medium-low, cover the saucepan, and cook for 20 minutes. Turn off the heat, fluff the rice with a fork, and serve.

WITH SO MANY highly flavored dishes on the dinner table, sometimes it's nice to have a salt-neutral starch to meld with and not fight against other flavors. Use the widest saucepan you have to cook the rice; the wider the pan, the better and fluffier the rice, since it has room to breathe and expand.

coconut rice

SERVES 8

¼ cup canola oil
1 medium red onion, thinly sliced
12 curry leaves, roughly torn (optional)
1 tablespoon mustard seeds
2 teaspoons cumin seeds

2 cups basmati rice
¼ cup unsweetened shredded coconut
3 cups water
1 cup coconut milk
1½ tablespoons kosher salt

Heat the oil with the onions, curry leaves (if using), mustard seeds, and cumin seeds in a large pot over medium-high heat, stirring occasionally, until the cumin is browned, about 2 minutes. Stir in the rice, cook for 2 minutes, and then mix in the coconut and cook, while stirring, until the coconut is fragrant, about 30 seconds to 1 minute. Add the water, coconut milk, and kosher salt and bring to a boil. Reduce the heat to low, cover the pot, and cook the rice for 20 minutes. Turn off the heat, fluff the rice with a fork, and serve.

THINK OF THIS as Indian fried rice. It's popular in southern India where various aromatic seeds and herbs are melded together to create inspired rice dishes. You can vary this recipe an infinite number of ways by replacing the coconut milk with an extra cup of water and trading shredded coconut for chopped radishes, tomatoes, lemon zest, yogurt, or even toasted peanuts.

tamarind rice

SERVES 8

1 tablespoon plus 1½ teaspoons
  tamarind concentrate
½ cup warm water
3 tablespoons canola oil
½ cup unsalted peanuts (preferably
  unroasted), roughly chopped
1 tablespoon mustard seeds
16 curry leaves, roughly torn (optional)
6 dried red chiles (optional)
1 teaspoon cumin seeds

¾ teaspoon turmeric
1 large red onion, quartered and thinly
  sliced
1 tablespoon plus 1 teaspoon kosher salt
2 teaspoons Sambhaar (page 21),
  or 1 teaspoon curry powder
7 cups cooked basmati rice, drained,
  spread out on a baking sheet, and
  cooled to room temperature

Place the tamarind in a small bowl and pour the warm water over it. Whisk together until the tamarind is completely dissolved and set aside.

Heat the oil, peanuts, and mustard seeds in a large skillet or pot over medium-high heat until the mustard seeds begin to pop, 2 to 3 minutes. Add the curry leaves, chiles, cumin, and turmeric and cook until the peanuts are golden, about 1½ minutes. Add the onion, salt, and Sambhaar and cook until the onion is soft, 4 to 5 minutes, stirring often (if the onion begins to burn, turn the heat down). Add the tamarind water and cook until the water is evaporated, stirring often, for about 2 minutes.

Stir in the rice and cook until the rice is hot, about 2 minutes (if the rice was in the refrigerator it will take an extra 2 to 4 minutes to warm up), stirring once or twice to make sure nothing burns at the bottom of the pan. Taste for seasoning and serve.

THIS IS A GOOD ACCOMPANIMENT to mild foods. The Sambhaar seasons the rice and leaves a tingle that lingers on your palate long after you've eaten. You can buy sambhaar powder in Indian markets or make your own with the recipe on page 21. In a pinch, use curry powder. If you like a sour flavor, add an extra 1½ teaspoons of tamarind concentrate to the rice.

pearl couscous with tomatoes

SERVES 4 TO 6

2 tablespoons extra-virgin olive oil

1 dried red chile

½ cinnamon stick

½ teaspoon ground peppercorns

2 medium red onions, quartered and thinly sliced

2 teaspoons kosher salt

3 medium tomatoes, chopped

1 cup large pearl couscous

4 cups water

1 tablespoon unsalted butter

Heat the oil with the chile, cinnamon, and ground peppercorns in a large skillet over medium-high heat until the cinnamon starts to unfurl, 2½ to 3 minutes. Add the onions and salt and cook, stirring often, until the onions are soft, about 3 minutes. Add the tomatoes and cook until they're thick and jammy, stirring often, about 5 minutes.

Stir in the couscous and cook for 1 minute, and then pour in 1 cup of water. Once the water comes to a simmer, reduce the heat to medium. Cook until the couscous sticks to the bottom of the skillet and the water is absorbed, stirring occasionally and scraping the bottom of the skillet in a back-and-forth motion for 3 to 4 minutes. Add another cup of water and cook until the water is absorbed, still stirring and scraping the pan, for 5 to 6 minutes. Add the remaining cup of water and cook until the water is absorbed, stirring and scraping occasionally, 7 to 8 minutes. Add 1 more cup of water and cook until the couscous is very sticky, stirring and scraping in a back-and-forth motion occasionally for about 10 minutes. Turn the heat to its lowest setting and cook 2 minutes longer. Cover the skillet and turn off the heat. Let the couscous sit 5 minutes and then serve.

MADE IN THE RISOTTO STYLE, pearl couscous (sometimes called Israeli couscous) has a great toothsome pastalike quality and is creamy and outrageously tasty. It's excellent as a side dish, or can be served on its own or with some added Parmigiano-Reggiano cheese, some broiled shrimp, or pan-seared scallops. For even more depth of flavor, use vegetable, chicken, or beef stock instead of water.

grandma hayes's corn bread

MAKES ONE 9-INCH SKILLET OF CORN BREAD

½ cup (1 stick) unsalted butter, cut into
    8 pieces
2 cups fresh corn kernels (cut from about
    3 ears)
1 small onion, finely chopped
¼ pound Parmigiano-Reggiano cheese,
    finely grated
1 package Jiffy corn muffin mix
⅓ cup all-purpose flour

½ cup chopped fresh cilantro
1 jalapeño (cored and seeded if you prefer
    a milder flavor), sliced into thin rings
½ teaspoon kosher salt
¼ teaspoon cayenne pepper
¼ teaspoon ground peppercorns
1 large egg, lightly beaten
⅔ cup fat-free plain yogurt

Preheat the oven to 400°F and set an oven rack at the lowest position. Melt the butter in a 9-inch cast-iron skillet over medium-high heat. Once melted, reduce the heat to low.

Place the corn, onion, cheese, corn muffin mix, flour, cilantro, jalapeño, salt, cayenne pepper, and ground peppercorns in a large bowl. In a medium bowl, lightly whisk together the egg and yogurt, then add it to the corn mixture, stirring until just combined and some dry patches remain (the consistency will be thick).

Pour the corn bread batter into the hot skillet and use a rubber spatula to press the batter into the pan. The butter will rise up the sides of skillet and over the top of the batter. Tilt the skillet toward you, and then rotate it away from you to coat the top of the batter evenly with melted butter. Bake the corn bread until its top is golden brown and a cake tester comes out clean, 30 to 35 minutes (some butter will still be bubbling around the edges of the skillet). Remove the skillet from the oven and set it aside to cool for at least 5 minutes before slicing and serving.

GRANDMA HAYES in West Virginia taught me how to make cast-iron skillet corn bread. By adding some Indian spices and seasonings, I've adjusted her recipe to reflect my cooking style. This corn bread has become a staple in my home and a favorite of many of my friends. To add a smoky edge, roast the corn over a high flame on your gas cooktop or on a baking sheet under the broiler before combining the kernels with the other corn bread ingredients.

grilling

India has a long tradition of grilling, and tandoori grilling has been a part of our world since the dawn of civilizations. A tandoor is a freestanding cylindrical clay oven that is wide at its belly and narrow at its top. A fire is built in the bottom of the pot and food that has been threaded onto long skewers is lowered into the oven. The tandoor cooks food at a very high heat—somewhere between 550°F and 850°F—which sears the outside of what is cooking while sealing in the juices. As the craft of tandoori grilling was honed throughout the centuries in ancient Persia, Pakistan, Turkey, and Afghanistan, its applications became more varied and its users more capable. Over time, India has developed its own tandoori cooking style that is considered one of the best traditions of grilling. Light in fat and bold in flavor, tandoori cooking is an easy way to prepare perfectly cooked and intensely flavored meats, poultry, and fish.

When diners experience the tandoori-grilled foods at my restaurant, they are often surprised to discover that the food is not neon orange or red in color, but instead has a beautiful charred finish that is just as natural as any grilled chicken.

Of course few of us have a tandoor in our backyard, so this chapter introduces recipes for the grill created in the tandoori style, like Chaat Masala Corn with Lime, a staple in India during the monsoon season, and Hemant's Famous Lamb Chops, a creation of my chef-partner, Hemant Mathur. Those who are addicted to grilled burgers will go wild for intensely flavored lamb burgers—in fact, they may never find satisfaction in a plain grilled beef burger again!

If you get seriously hooked on grilling with an Indian flavor (and this is easy to do); consider purchasing a tandoor, which will cook food in less time and with even better results than you'll get from a charcoal or gas grill. I owned a tandoor when I lived in the West Village in Manhattan. Barbecuing on the patio, surrounded with friends, brought me back to India where tandoori cooking was once a community event, with women gathering for a social hour while baking fresh parathas and naans for their families. Conversations took place around the tandoor, gossip started from here, and spice was added to the duller moments of life. Grilling is similarly a great way to entertain while preparing a feast, bringing together people of different nationalities and backgrounds for one purpose—deeply satisfying food.

chaat masala corn with lime

MAKES 8 EARS

8 ears of corn, shucked
2 limes, cut into wedges

¼ cup chaat masala
Cayenne pepper, for sprinkling (optional)

Preheat the grill to medium-high (you should be able to hold your hand 5 inches above the grate for no more than 3 to 4 seconds). Cook the corn, turning often, until it is browned on all sides (it's good to have some charred kernels), 10 to 15 minutes.

Place the corn on a platter. Dip a lime wedge in the chaat masala and rub into the corn, squeezing the wedge slightly to get some juice into the kernels. Repeat, dipping the lime into the chaat masala and rubbing all over the corn until it is seasoned to your liking. Sprinkle with cayenne pepper (if using) and eat while hot.

THIS IS ONE of my all-time favorite ways to eat corn. I remember as a child, how my sister and I would wait for my father's car to appear at the side of the road that led to our house at the end of the day. The very second we saw his car, we'd run full speed to buy this corn, which is best eaten right off the grill, from a street vendor. We were proud to present Dad this welcome-home offering every day during the monsoon season, when corn is harvested. We ate the corn fast and silently, trying to beat the omnipresent threat of rain, often returning to the street vendor only minutes after our first visit to buy a second helping. Though the corn won't have quite the same grilled flavor, you can also make it over a gas burner.

grilled vegetable salad

SERVES 8

FOR THE MARINADE

¼ cup balsamic vinegar

3 garlic cloves, peeled and finely minced

A 1-inch piece fresh ginger, peeled and finely minced

¾ cup extra-virgin olive oil

1 teaspoon kosher salt

½ teaspoon ground peppercorns

¼ cup chopped fresh cilantro leaves plus ¼ cup chopped leaves, for serving

¼ cup chopped fresh mint leaves

¼ teaspoon cayenne pepper

¼ teaspoon ground coriander

¼ teaspoon Garam Masala (page 20)

FOR THE SALAD

12 cherry tomatoes

1 red onion, quartered lengthwise

1 zucchini, quartered lengthwise

1 yellow summer squash, quartered lengthwise

1 red bell pepper, quartered, cored, and seeded

1 yellow bell pepper, quartered, cored, and seeded

1 green bell pepper, quartered, cored, and seeded

8 asparagus spears, tough ends removed

Cilantro, for sprinkling

To make the marinade, whisk the vinegar, garlic, and ginger together in a large bowl. Whisk in the oil, salt, and ground peppercorns and then mix in the remaining marinade ingredients. Pour a quarter of the marinade into a small bowl and set aside. Add the vegetables to the large bowl of marinade and toss to coat. Let the vegetables marinate while you heat the grill.

Preheat the grill to medium-high (you should be able to hold your hand 5 inches above the grate for no more than 3 to 4 seconds). Thread the cherry tomatoes onto metal skewers and the onion quarters onto different metal skewers. Place the skewers and all of the other vegetables on the grill and cook until charred and tender, removing the vegetables from the grill as they are finished cooking (they will be done cooking at different times, the tomatoes requiring the least time to grill and the onion requiring the most). Cut the grilled zucchini, squash, bell peppers, and onions into 2-inch pieces and slice the asparagus spears in half crosswise. Place all of the vegetables in a large bowl and toss with the reserved marinade. Taste for seasoning, sprinkle with cilantro, and serve.

COLORFUL AND DELICIOUS, this grilled salad is a must for barbecues and picnics. Add or subtract vegetables as you like. Some other vegetables that are nice on the grill include wedges of fennel or radicchio and rounds of eggplant. You can even add fruit, like peaches, nectarines, pineapples, pears, and apples if you like.

creamy vegetable burgers

MAKES 8 BURGERS

1 pound red potatoes

1 medium carrot, peeled and quartered

1 small tomato, quartered

1 small red onion, quartered

1 jalapeño (cored and seeded if you prefer a milder flavor), quartered

1 (15-ounce) can chickpeas, drained and rinsed

1 cup roughly chopped fresh cilantro

1 teaspoon Garam Masala (page 20)

1 teaspoon amchur powder (optional)

¼ teaspoon cayenne pepper

2 teaspoons kosher salt

½ teaspoon ground peppercorns

1 cup dry bread crumbs

Canola oil, for greasing grill grates

¼ cup extra-virgin olive oil

8 hamburger buns or pita bread

Bring a large pot of water to a boil. Add the potatoes and boil until they are knife tender, 30 to 40 minutes, depending on their size. Drain, cool, peel, quarter, and set aside.

Place all of the remaining ingredients except for the bread crumbs, oils, and buns into the bowl of a food processor and process until fine. Add the potatoes and pulse to incorporate. Transfer the mixture to a bowl, cover with plastic wrap, and refrigerate for at least 2 hours or overnight (chilling makes the mixture easier to handle).

Place the bread crumbs in a shallow dish. Form the mixture into 8 equal and thick patties and gently press each in bread crumbs, coating the patty on all sides. Place the patties on a plate, cover with plastic wrap, and refrigerate for at least 2 hours or up to overnight (at this point, the patties can be placed on a baking sheet and frozen; after freezing, individually wrap in plastic wrap and place in resealable plastic bags for up to 2 months).

Preheat the grill to medium-high (you should be able to hold your hand 5 inches above the grate for no more than 3 to 4 seconds). Pour some canola oil into a small bowl. Wad up a couple paper towels and dip them into the oil. Using tongs, rub the oiled paper towels onto the grill grate to grease it. Brush one side of each patty with some olive oil and place the oiled side on the grill. Brush the top of the patty with more olive oil. Cook without moving until each side is browned and crisp, 4 to 6 minutes per side (if you move the patty, it will lose its crust and may crumble). Serve on buns or in pita with ketchup.

VEGETARIANS IN INDIA aren't interested in replicating the flavor or texture of meat, so when you bite into this burger and encounter its creamy, soft texture, don't be surprised! These burgers are excellent topped with any kind of chutney, grilled onions, or roasted peppers. Or do as I do and eat on a soft bun with lots and lots of ketchup. They are just as tasty pan-fried in canola oil.

grilled tuna steaks with garam masala and lime

SERVES 4

2 tablespoons plus 1½ teaspoons
   sesame oil
1 tablespoons honey
Juice of 1 lime plus 1 lime cut into
   wedges, for serving
6 garlic cloves, peeled and finely minced
3 teaspoons kosher salt

½ teaspoon Garam Masala (page 20)
½ teaspoon ground ginger
¼ teaspoon cayenne pepper
½ teaspoon ground peppercorns
4 tuna steaks (6 to 8 ounces each) of even
   thickness
Canola oil, for greasing grill grates

Mix the sesame oil, honey, lime juice, garlic, 2 teaspoons of salt, Garam Masala, ginger, cayenne pepper, and ground peppercorns together in a gallon-sized resealable plastic bag. Add the tuna and turn to coat; then refrigerate for 30 minutes or up to 4 hours.

Preheat the grill to medium-high (you should be able to hold your hand 5 inches above the grate for no more than 3 to 4 seconds). Pour some canola oil into a small bowl. Wad up a couple of paper towels and dip them into the oil. Using tongs, rub the oiled paper towels onto the grill grate to grease it. Sprinkle the tuna steaks with the remaining 1 teaspoon of salt and grill for 4 minutes, or until they have char marks and are golden on one side. Turn the steaks over, cover with the grill cover or with a disposable aluminum pan, and cook for an additional 3 to 5 minutes (3 minutes for rare, 5 minutes for medium). Serve with lime wedges.

WHEN SHOPPING for tuna steaks, be sure to select steaks of the same shape and thickness so they cook at the same rate on the grill. Cook tuna steaks so that they are still rare in the middle, and then slice them at an angle and shingle over a salad for a stunning presentation.

jumbo shrimp masala

SERVES 4

2 tablespoons lime juice plus 1 lime cut into wedges, for serving

16 garlic cloves, peeled and finely minced

1 teaspoon cumin seeds

1 teaspoon Garam Masala (page 20)

1 teaspoon ground peppercorns

½ teaspoon Toasted Cumin (page 16)

½ teaspoon ground ginger

½ teaspoon turmeric

2 cups sour cream

12 "colossal" shrimp (about 2 pounds), peeled and deveined

Canola oil, for greasing grill grates

2 teaspoons kosher salt

3 tablespoons unsalted butter, melted

¼ teaspoon chaat masala (optional)

Whisk the lime juice with the garlic and spices in a large bowl. Add the sour cream, whisking until smooth, and pour into a gallon-sized resealable plastic bag. Add the shrimp and turn to coat. Refrigerate for at least 2 hours or up to overnight (if marinating overnight, they will grill more quickly as the marinade slightly "cooks" the shrimp).

Preheat the grill to medium-high (you should be able to hold your hand 5 inches above the grate for no more than 3 to 4 seconds). Pour some canola oil into a small bowl. Wad up a couple of paper towels and dip them into the oil. Using tongs, rub the oiled paper towels onto the grill grate to grease it. Remove the shrimp from the marinade and thread them onto skewers. Sprinkle the shrimp with salt and grill until they start to turn red, about 3 minutes on each side. Remove the skewers from the grill and let the shrimp rest on a baking sheet for 5 minutes. Brush them with the melted butter and grill until each side is a little charred, another 1 or 2 minutes on each side. Sprinkle the shrimp with chaat masala (if using) and serve with lime wedges.

THESE SHRIMP are a staple at my New York City restaurant. People never stop talking about them once they have tried them. Tender and intensely flavorful, it is worth searching out large tiger shrimp (also called "colossal" shrimp) for this recipe—they are that much more impressive served from the skewer. The marinade used here is a classic Indian recipe that works well with other kinds of steaklike fish such as halibut. Jumbo Shrimp Masala is wonderful with Crispy Okra Salad (page 65).

tandoori chicken with ginger and spices

SERVES 4

FOR THE CHICKEN

Juice of 1 lemon plus 1 lemon, cut into
   wedges
1 tablespoon paprika
1 teaspoon kosher salt
¼ teaspoon turmeric
1 chicken (3½ to 4 pounds), skin
   removed, cut into 8 or 10 pieces

FOR THE MARINADE

1 small red onion, quartered
4 garlic cloves, peeled and roughly
   chopped
A 2-inch piece ginger, peeled and roughly
   chopped
½ cup sour cream

3 tablespoons tomato paste, or
   1½ tablespoons concentrated tomato
   paste
1 teaspoon ground coriander
1 teaspoon Toasted Cumin (page 16)
1 teaspoon ground peppercorns
¾ teaspoon ground cardamom
½ teaspoon cayenne pepper
½ teaspoon paprika
Pinch of ground cloves
Pinch of ground cinnamon
Pinch of Garam Masala (page 20)

2 tablespoons canola oil
1 lemon, cut into wedges for serving

To prepare the chicken, mix the lemon juice, paprika, salt, and turmeric together in a large bowl. Cut several diagonal slashes in each piece of chicken, taking care not to cut down to the bone. Add the chicken to the bowl and rub with the spices. Cover with plastic wrap and set aside for 30 minutes.

To make the marinade, place all of the ingredients in a food processor and pulse until smooth. Pour over the chicken and toss to coat with the marinade and then divide the chicken between two resealable plastic bags. Refrigerate for at least 4 hours or up to 2 days.

Preheat half of the grill to medium-high (you should be able to hold your hand 5 inches above the grate for no more than 3 to 4 seconds) and the other half to medium-low (you should be able to hold your hand 5 inches above the grate for 6 to 7 seconds).

Add 1 tablespoon of oil to each bag of chicken, reseal, and massage to incorporate. Remove the chicken from the marinade and place on the hot portion of the grill, cooking until each side is browned, 2 to 4 minutes per side. Transfer the chicken pieces to the cool side of the grill, cover with the grill cover or a disposable aluminum pan, and cook 20 to 25 minutes or until cooked through. Move the chicken to a platter and let stand 5 minutes before serving with lemon wedges.

FOR THE BEST FLAVOR, the chicken should be marinated overnight, but in a pinch you can marinate it for as little as 4 hours. I simplify the classic recipe by using sour cream instead of traditional strained yogurt, which must be hung in cheesecloth to drain overnight. Be forewarned: Unlike the typical restaurant tandoori, the chicken will not be a bright red color since no food coloring or other artificial ingredients are added to the marinade.

honey-glazed double-thick pork chops

SERVES 4 TO 8

¼ cup extra-virgin olive oil
⅓ cup honey
2 tablespoons balsamic vinegar
1 teaspoon chopped fresh rosemary
1 teaspoon chopped fresh thyme leaves

½ teaspoon cayenne pepper (optional)
1 teaspoon kosher salt
½ teaspoon ground peppercorns
4 pork loin chops, 1½ inches thick

Whisk the oil, honey, vinegar, rosemary, thyme, cayenne pepper (if using), salt, and ground peppercorns in a small bowl. Transfer to a gallon-sized resealable plastic bag, add the chops, and turn to coat in the marinade. Refrigerate for at least 4 hours or up to overnight.

Preheat half of your grill to medium-high (you should be able to hold your hand 5 inches above the grate for no more than 3 to 4 seconds) and the other half to medium-low (you should be able to hold your hand 5 inches above the grate for 6 to 7 seconds). Sear the pork chops on the hot side of the grill until charred, 2 to 3 minutes on each side (have a water bottle handy in case there are any flare-ups). Slide the chops to the cool side of the grill, cover with the grill cover or a disposable aluminum pan, and grill 12 to 15 minutes or until its temperature registers between 160°F and 165°F. Serve immediately.

THIS IS A "WOW" DISH. Serve it at a party or to a date for instant accolades. Overnight marinating makes the pork chops extra flavorful and juicy. The chops are big enough to serve 1 or 2 people each. If you use a charcoal grill, bank the charcoal so there is more coal on one side, creating a hotter side and a cooler one. You can also use a grill pan to make the pork chops indoors.

lamb burgers with cilantro-yogurt sauce

SERVES 6

FOR THE CILANTRO-YOGURT SAUCE
3 tablespoons fresh lemon juice
4 jalapeños, cored, seeded, and minced
2 cups fresh cilantro, roughly chopped
A 2-inch piece fresh ginger, peeled and
  roughly chopped
1 tablespoon sugar
1 small red onion, finely chopped
1 teaspoon kosher salt
¾ cup plain yogurt

FOR THE BURGERS
2½ pounds ground lamb
6 scallions (white and light green parts
  only), finely chopped
½ cup finely chopped fresh mint leaves
½ cup grated Parmigiano-Reggiano
  cheese

Zest of 2 lemons
2 teaspoons lemon juice
2 teaspoons kosher salt
½ teaspoon ground peppercorns
¼ teaspoon cayenne pepper

FOR THE SALAD TOPPING
1 medium tomato, thinly sliced
1 small cucumber, peeled, halved, seeded,
  and thinly sliced
Onion reserved from the yogurt sauce
1 tablespoon plus 1 teaspoon lemon juice
1 teaspoon kosher salt
¼ teaspoon ground peppercorns

6 rolls, split and toasted on the grill

To make the sauce, in a food processor combine the lemon juice, half of the jalapeños, the cilantro, ginger, sugar, half of the finely chopped onion, and salt and process until fine. Transfer to a small bowl, cover with plastic wrap, and refrigerate.

To prepare the burgers, preheat the grill to medium-high (you should be able to hold your hand 5 inches above the grate for no more than 3 to 4 seconds). While it heats, combine the ground lamb with the remaining jalapeños, the scallions, mint, cheese, lemon zest, and lemon juice in a large bowl. Add the salt, ground peppercorns, and the cayenne pepper and mix with your hands. Pat the meat into 6 burgers and set aside.

To make the salad topping, toss the tomato, cucumber, and remaining chopped onion together in a medium bowl. Add the lemon juice, salt, and ground peppercorns.

Grill the burgers until nicely charred on the outside and pink within, 5 to 8 minutes per side. Fold the yogurt into the cilantro sauce. Spread some of this sauce on the bottom half of each roll. Top with a burger, another dollop of sauce, and some of the tomato-cucumber salad. Cover with the other bun half and serve.

I DEVELOPED THIS BURGER recipe for a story about America's best burgers that ran in *Food & Wine* magazine in August 2004. The title of the story was "The Great Burger Challenge," and my burger was one of the staff favorites. These burgers have all of the nuance and sophistication that you would expect from Indian cuisine yet are easy to make and cook. Served with a chopped salad (page 58), it becomes a fast, flavorful, and cooling dinner.

lamb seekh kebabs

SERVES 8

2½ pounds ground lamb
½ cup dried apricots or figs, soaked in warm water 10 minutes, drained and finely chopped
1 small red onion, finely chopped
6 scallions (green and white parts only), finely chopped
2 jalapeños, cored, seeded, and finely chopped

½ cup finely chopped fresh mint leaves
¼ cup finely chopped fresh cilantro
Zest and juice of 1 lemon
1 tablespoon Garam Masala (page 20)
1½ teaspoons kosher salt
½ teaspoon ground peppercorns
½ teaspoon cayenne pepper

Preheat the grill to a medium-high heat (you should be able to hold your hand 5 inches above the grate for no more than 3 to 4 seconds).

In a large bowl, combine the ground lamb with the apricots, onion, scallions, jalapeños, mint, cilantro, and lemon zest and juice. Add the Garam Masala, salt, ground peppercorns, and cayenne pepper and mix gently. Divide the meat into eight equal portions. Form each into a short, thick cylinder and thread one onto each skewer. Squeeze and pat the meat to lengthen on the skewer. Grill until browned, about 4 minutes per side (note that even when cooked, the kebabs will still be pink inside), and serve.

SEEKH IS THE HINDI word for "skewer." These kebabs are a mainstay of most tandoori kitchens. For another layer of flavor, add ½ teaspoon of coarsely ground fennel seeds to the mix. This recipe can be used to make lamb burgers that are delicious on a bun or stuffed into pita pockets with Indian Chopped Mixed Salad (page 58).

hemant's famous lamb chops

SERVES 4

8 to 10 lamb rib chops (about 2 pounds), cut 1 to 1½ inches thick

1 cup yogurt, drained in a cheesecloth-lined strainer or coffee filter for 2 to 4 hours, or 1 cup sour cream or crème fraîche

¼ cup malt vinegar

Juice of 1 lemon

8 garlic cloves, peeled and finely minced

A 3-inch piece fresh ginger, peeled and grated

1 tablespoon Garam Masala (page 20)

1 tablespoon Toasted Cumin (page 16)

1 teaspoon ground cardamom

½ teaspoon cayenne pepper

¼ teaspoon ground mace

¼ teaspoon ground nutmeg

2 tablespoons canola oil

3 tablespoons unsalted butter, melted

Cut 3 or 4 deep slashes in each of the lamb chops, taking care not to cut all the way through the chop. Mix the yogurt, vinegar, lemon juice, garlic, ginger, Garam Masala, Toasted Cumin, cardamom, cayenne pepper, mace, and nutmeg in a gallon-sized resealable plastic bag. Add the chops, then turn to coat them in marinade, and refrigerate for 4 hours or up to overnight.

Preheat your grill to a medium-high heat (you should be able to hold your hand 5 inches above the grate for no more than 3 to 4 seconds). Add the oil to the bag, reseal, and massage the chops to incorporate. Remove the lamb from the marinade, place on the grill, and cook for 4 to 5 minutes on each side. Transfer to a baking sheet and let the lamb rest for 5 minutes. Brush with melted butter and return to the grill, until each side is evenly browned, about 5 more minutes per side, and serve.

THIS RECIPE HIGHLIGHTS the tandoor talents of chef Hemant Mathur, my long-time friend, confidant, and chef-partner. The lamb chops are our interpretation of the amazing ones served at Karim's, a food stall in Old Delhi, near the Jama Masjid Mosque, which is the largest in India. Hemant's lamb chops have since become the absolute best-seller at the restaurant. Be sure to drain the yogurt for at least 2 hours before using or the lamb will never develop its signature savory crust during cooking. In a pinch, you can use sour cream or créme fraîche instead.

breakfasts

In my family, breakfast was always a treat to wake up to. My father called breakfast the "breaking of fast," and Panditji, the family chef, would take my father's translation and the preparation of this meal to heart. Potato-and-Pea Poha, Toasty Postys, or spicy scrambled eggs were just a few of his specialties. Whenever Panditji went on vacation, and while my family lived in Nagpur for three years and summered in the Hill Stations, Mom would take over breakfast duty. Not one to ever be outdone by anyone else, her French Toast and Savory Indian Crêpes with Tomato-Shallot Chutney were often highlights of our summer vacation.

The Hindi word for breakfast is nashta, a term that can also be used to describe a snack (it has always struck me as curious how close in pronunciation and meaning nashta is to the Yiddish word for snacking, *nosh*). My family enjoyed the recipes in this chapter for breakfast but also as afternoon snacks and late-night meals. In the same vein, dishes from other chapters that aren't traditionally considered breakfast items—like Aloo Bonda Potato Dumplings (page 38) and Vegetable Burgers (page 195) were often served as our morning meal. I encourage you to try adding some of these savory egg-free dishes to your morning routine.

Since I began living on my own, I've come to realize that breakfast is the perfect time of day to entertain, and breaking of the fast soon became my weekend ritual. I invite people over around noon and cook throughout the morning, bringing new dishes out of the kitchen every so often, taking time out from cooking to chat with guests.

Some of the recipes that follow will seem esoteric or exotic, but once you are beyond the stage of prepping and into the cooking process, you will realize how comforting, simple, and accessible these recipes are. The Toasty Postys take simple scrambled eggs and make them into Italian-style paninis that are scrumptious. I could eat them for breakfast, lunch, and dinner and never tire of them (and often I just do that). The Mixed Vegetable Frittata supplies a breakfast that is satisfying for many reasons in addition to its flavor—it's a one-dish meal that feeds a crowd.

Cheelas and French toast were two of my favorite dishes that Mom made while I was growing up. I picked up my technique for French toast from her, the world's best French toast maker. As a child, I remember her cooking them effortlessly, and yet we kids savored each bite. **Indian breakfast crêpes are my Indian heritage at its culinary peak.** Made with almost zero work, they are so good that you could easily eat one too many—and then not be able to eat for hours. Mom makes them to this day, and they are still absolutely brilliant.

toasty postys (indian panini)

MAKES 4 SANDWICHES

4 large eggs

1 jalapeño (cored and seeded if you prefer a milder flavor), diced

3 tablespoons chopped fresh cilantro

1/8 teaspoon Garam Masala (page 20)

1/2 teaspoon kosher salt

1/2 teaspoon ground peppercorns

2 tablespoons canola oil

1 small red onion, diced

1 small tomato (preferably a plum tomato), diced

1/4 pound Gouda cheese, sliced into 8 pieces

8 slices sandwich bread

Ketchup, for serving (optional)

Whisk the eggs, jalapeño, cilantro, Garam Masala, salt, and 1/4 teaspoon of the ground peppercorns in a medium bowl and set aside.

Heat the oil and the remaining 1/4 teaspoon pepper in a medium nonstick skillet over medium-high heat until the peppercorns sizzle, about 2 minutes. Add the onion and cook, stirring often, until it is soft and barely translucent, about 2 minutes. Add the diced tomato and the egg mixture. Move a nonstick spatula in a back-and-forth motion along the pan's bottom to gently rake the eggs into semisoft curds, cooking for 1 1/2 to 2 minutes or longer if you like your eggs well done. Remove the scrambled eggs from the heat and set aside.

Heat a sandwich press according to the manufacturer's instructions. Place 1 slice of Gouda on each of 4 slices of bread. Cover with a heaping 1/4 cup of eggs, top with another slice of Gouda, and cover with a slice of bread. Toast the sandwiches until they're browned, 2 to 3 minutes (the cooking time will vary depending on your sandwich press). Cut into quarters and serve with ketchup if you like.

ON SUNDAYS PANDITJI, my family's now-retired chef in New Delhi, would make ande kee bhojia, or scrambled eggs. If he was in the mood to spoil us, he would turn the scrambled eggs into Toasty Posty sandwiches. We didn't have a panini press back then; instead Panditji toasted the sandwich in a square metal cage over an open flame until it was slightly charred. The potential for variations on this sandwich are limitless. I've been known to add a layer of leftover mashed potatoes or leftover stir-fried vegetables to the sandwich. If you don't have a sandwich press, brush the Toasty Posty with melted butter and brown in a skillet as you would a grilled cheese sandwich. Or eliminate the bread all together and enjoy as wonderfully spiced scrambled eggs.

telouet omelet

SERVES 8

FOR THE OMELET
12 large eggs
¼ cup chopped fresh cilantro
½ teaspoon Aleppo pepper, or ¼ teaspoon cayenne pepper
¼ teaspoon Garam Masala (page 20)
1 teaspoon kosher salt
¼ teaspoon ground peppercorns

FOR THE VEGETABLES
6 tablespoons extra-virgin olive oil
1 teaspoon cumin seeds
½ teaspoon red pepper flakes
2 medium red onions, halved and thickly sliced

1 tablespoon plus 2 teaspoons kosher salt
½ teaspoon cayenne (optional)
¼ teaspoon ground peppercorns
5 garlic cloves, peeled
½ teaspoon turmeric
2 red bell peppers, cored, seeded, and thickly sliced
2 yellow bell peppers, cored, seeded, and thickly sliced
2 green bell peppers, cored, seeded, and thickly sliced
2 teaspoons honey
3 large tomatoes, thinly sliced
Juice of ½ lemon
8 pieces pita bread

To prepare the omelet, beat all of the ingredients together in a large bowl and set aside.

Prepare the vegetables: Heat the oil with the cumin seeds in a large skillet over medium-high heat until the cumin becomes toasty and browned, about 2 minutes. Add the pepper flakes and cook for 30 seconds, then mix in the onions, salt, cayenne pepper (if using), and ground peppercorns. Cook, stirring often, until the onions are soft, about 3 minutes. Add the garlic cloves and the turmeric and cook until the garlic is fragrant, about 1 minute, and then mix in the bell peppers. Cook the peppers for 2 minutes and then stir in the honey and cook for another 2 minutes. Cover the skillet, reduce the heat to medium-low, and cook for 10 minutes, stirring halfway through. Add the tomatoes and increase the heat to medium-high. Cover and cook for another 10 minutes, stirring every few minutes to break up the tomatoes.

Remove the cover and cook the juices down until they're jammy and thick, anywhere from 3 to 10 minutes depending on how juicy your tomatoes were. Stir in the lemon juice and then pour the eggs over the vegetables. Reduce the heat to medium and cook, covered, until the omelet is completely cooked through, 12 to 15 minutes. Serve in wedges with warmed pita bread.

BEFORE KING HASSAN DIED, I was a guest of the Moroccan government at an annual sacred music festival in Fez. After the festival, I decided to drive up to the High Atlas Mountains with a friend and two local men who served as our guides and translators. The guides told us about an amazing old town called Telouet, and we decided to stay there overnight at a bed and breakfast. Unfortunately the bed and breakfast was closed; the chef, however, invited us to his home for lunch. Within 45 minutes he served us an omelet made in a tagine, explaining that it is a classic winter dish usually made roadside over coals by Berber tribals. Its saucy base of mixed bell peppers, onions, and tomatoes is covered with beaten eggs that form an omelet-like layer on top. It was hands-down one of the best meals I had in Morocco. Here, the ras al hanout used to spice the eggs is replaced by Garam Masala and some other spices like cumin, red pepper flakes, turmeric, and garlic. Delicious and exotic, this is something I probably eat for dinner perhaps more often than I do for breakfast. Be sure to serve with plenty of pita bread.

mixed vegetable frittata

SERVES 8

1 large tomato, sliced into 8 rounds
16 fresh basil leaves
10 large eggs
1 tablespoon plus ½ teaspoon kosher salt
1 teaspoon ground peppercorns
2 cups grated Parmigiano-Reggiano cheese
¼ cup extra-virgin olive oil
½ teaspoon chopped fresh thyme leaves
¼ teaspoon red pepper flakes

18 scallions (white part only), thinly sliced
2 shallots, peeled and thinly sliced
3 red bell peppers, cored, seeded, halved
    widthwise, and thinly sliced
2 pounds asparagus, tough ends
    removed, cut into 2-inch lengths
9 ounces baby spinach
¾-pound ball of fresh unsalted
    mozzarella, sliced into 8 rounds

Preheat the oven to 425°F. Lay the tomato slices on a paper towel–lined plate. Cover with another paper towel and gently press to absorb extra moisture and set aside. Stack 8 of the basil leaves, roll lengthwise and cut crosswise into thin strips, and set aside. Whisk the eggs, ½ teaspoon kosher salt, ½ teaspoon ground peppercorns, and 1 cup of the Parmesan cheese together in a large bowl and set aside.

Heat the olive oil with the thyme, pepper flakes, and remaining ½ teaspoon ground pepper in an oven-safe large skillet or paella pan over medium-high heat and cook, stirring occasionally, until the thyme is fragrant and slightly fried, about 2 minutes. Add the scallions and shallots and cook until they're just starting to soften, about 1 minute. Add the bell peppers and remaining 1 tablespoon of salt and cook, stirring occasionally, until the peppers are soft but still al dente, about 6 minutes. Reduce the heat to medium and continue to cook until they're completely tender, about 4 minutes longer. Gently stir in the asparagus and spinach. Cook, stirring often until the spinach wilts, 3 to 3½ minutes. Increase the heat to medium-high and cook until most of the liquid is evaporated, stirring often, for anywhere from 2 to 6 minutes.

Pour the eggs over the vegetables, reduce the heat to low, and cook until you can see that the eggs are setting on top of the vegetables, about 5 minutes. Arrange the mozzarella slices on top of the eggs. Lay 1 basil leaf on top of each mozzarella slice and cover with a tomato slice. Sprinkle the sliced basil and the remaining 1 cup of Parmesan over the top of the frittata. Bake until the top of the frittata is browned and puffy, 18 to 20 minutes. Remove it from the oven and slice and serve immediately, or serve at room temperature.

FRITTATAS ARE ONE of my Sunday brunch staples. Use exciting colors to make the frittata attractive; a blend of red, green, and orange is always vibrant and enticing. Broil the frittata if you like it extra dark, and remember that a frittata keeps beautifully and can be eaten fresh from the oven, at room temperature, or reheated. If you can't find unsalted mozzarella, use salted mozzarella and reduce the kosher salt by 1 teaspoon.

indian shirred eggs with eggplant

SERVES 6

3 tablespoons unsalted butter, at room
  temperature, for greasing
1 recipe Indian Eggplant Caponata
  (page 39)
6 large eggs

Kosher salt and ground peppercorns
Toasted Cumin (page 16)
Good-quality extra-virgin olive oil
6 pieces buttered toast, cut into thirds

Preheat the oven to 450°F. Grease six small ramekins or shallow individual-sized gratin dishes with butter and set aside.

Place ⅓ cup (or more if you have larger ramekins or gratin dishes) of Indian Eggplant Caponata in each ramekin and make a deep well in the center of the eggplant. Crack an egg into the well and sprinkle it with salt, ground peppercorns, and Toasted Cumin. Place the ramekins in the oven and bake until the whites are cooked and the yolk is barely set, 10 to 14 minutes (or longer if you want your yolks completely cooked through). Drizzle with olive oil and serve with the buttered toast sticks.

THIS IS A BEAUTIFUL, elegant way to serve eggs for breakfast or brunch, in shallow individual gratin dishes or ramekins. Another fun option is to serve the shirred eggs in small, crusty rolls: Hollow out the roll, brush it inside and out with melted butter, and toast it until it is golden. Fill with a little Indian Eggplant Caponata and 1 egg and then bake as described above.

fried eggs with asparagus and prosciutto

SERVES 6

Wedge of Parmigiano-Reggiano cheese

2 pounds asparagus, tough ends removed

¼ cup plus 2 teaspoons extra-virgin olive oil plus extra, for drizzling

Zest of 1 lemon

1 teaspoon kosher salt

1 teaspoon ground peppercorns

⅓ pound thinly sliced prosciutto

6 large eggs

Set an oven rack at its uppermost position and preheat the broiler. Use a vegetable peeler to shave 16 thin ribbons of Parmesan from the wedge of cheese and set aside.

Place the asparagus on a rimmed baking sheet and drizzle with 3 tablespoons of oil. Sprinkle with the lemon zest, ½ teaspoon of the salt, and ½ teaspoon of the ground peppercorns. Broil the asparagus until it's tender, 10 to 12 minutes, shaking the pan 2 or 3 times.

Wrap 6 to 8 asparagus spears (depending on how thick they are) with 2 slices of prosciutto and place the bundles on individual plates or on a platter. Heat 1 teaspoon of oil in a large non-stick skillet over medium heat. Crack 3 eggs into the skillet, allowing the whites to set slightly before adding another egg to the pan. Sprinkle the eggs with salt and cracked peppercorns and cook until the white is set, 3 to 5 minutes. Slide a spatula under an egg and drape it over an asparagus bundle. Drizzle with olive oil and top with a couple of cheese ribbons. Repeat with the remaining eggs and asparagus bundles, adding the remaining teaspoon of oil, if necessary, to the skillet: serve hot.

THIS DISH WAS INSPIRED by a breakfast that I ate at a bistro in Paris consisting of sautéed asparagus topped with a radiant sunny-side-up duck egg. Its only garnish was freshly ground black pepper and coarse salt along with some good bread on the side. For extra elegance, drizzle some truffle oil over the eggs. If you're feeling really indulgent, grate fresh truffles over the eggs.

potato-and-pea poha

SERVES 6

¼ cup canola oil

1 teaspoon black mustard seeds

1 teaspoon cumin seeds

20 curry leaves, roughly torn (optional)

1 medium red onion, halved and thinly sliced

2 tablespoons kosher salt

2 small red potatoes, diced into very small cubes

½ teaspoon turmeric

1 jalapeño (cored and seeded if you prefer a milder flavor), finely diced

4 cups poha, rinsed in cold water and drained

1 cup frozen green peas

1 medium ripe tomato, cored and finely chopped

½ cup water

Juice of 1 lime plus 1 lime, cut into wedges, for serving

¾ cup chopped fresh cilantro

Heat the oil with the mustard seeds, cumin seeds, and curry leaves (if using) in a large skillet or wok over medium-high heat and cook, stirring often, until the cumin seeds are golden brown, about 2 minutes. Stir in the onion and salt and cook, stirring occasionally, until the onion is soft but not browned, 3 to 4 minutes. Add the potatoes and cook, stirring occasionally, for another 3 to 4 minutes. Add the turmeric and jalapeño and cook until the potatoes are tender and crispy browned, 5 to 6 minutes, stirring only once or twice.

Carefully stir in the poha, frozen peas, and tomato, taking care not to overwork and break the rice flakes. Once completely incorporated, drizzle the water around the edges of the skillet. Cover and reduce the heat to low, cooking the poha until it is completely tender, about 5 minutes. Add the lime juice and ½ cup of the cilantro and fluff with a fork. Taste for seasoning and serve sprinkled with the remaining cilantro and surrounded by lime wedges.

THROUGHOUT HIGH SCHOOL, my best friend, Mohit Jain, and I would compete with each other over whose family chef or mother made the best poha. When we felt generous, we'd shower the other's poha with accolades. At other times, we'd remain fiercely loyal to our own. Either way, poha always remained our favorite snack, sent with us to school in a classic stainless-steel tiffin box with a wedge of lime. Now that I'm grown, poha is a staple in my kitchen. When friends stop in craving something homey, or when my father, a fussy and loyal Indian food devotee, visits me in New York, I often prepare Potato-and-Pea Poha. It's simple and comforting and, given the chance, will become a staple in your kitchen, too.

savory indian crêpes with tomato-shallot chutney (cheelas)

SERVES 4 TO 6

FOR THE CRÊPES

1 cup chickpea flour (besan)

1 teaspoon kosher salt

½ teaspoon carom (ajowan)

⅛ teaspoon cayenne pepper

¾ cup water

1 jalapeño (cored and seeded if you prefer a milder flavor), finely chopped

¼ cup chopped fresh cilantro

1½ teaspoons canola oil

FOR THE CHUTNEY

1 tablespoon canola oil

4 large shallots, peeled and finely chopped

2 teaspoons kosher salt

3 medium tomatoes, finely chopped

1 jalapeño (cored and seeded if you prefer a milder flavor), finely chopped

½ cup chopped fresh cilantro

To prepare the crêpes, whisk the chickpea flour, salt, carom, and cayenne pepper together in a medium bowl. Whisk in the water (the batter should look like a thin pancake batter) and set the batter aside for 30 minutes.

While the batter rests, make the chutney: Heat the oil in a medium saucepan over medium-high heat for 1 minute. Add the shallots and salt and cook until the shallots are transparent, 2 to 3 minutes. Stir in the tomatoes, jalapeño, and cilantro, cover the saucepan, and reduce the heat to medium. Cook until the tomatoes are very saucy, 6 to 8 minutes. Uncover the saucepan and increase the heat to medium-high. Cook until the chutney is thick and jammy, another 6 to 8 minutes. Set it aside while you make the crêpes.

Gently stir the jalapeño and ¼ cup cilantro into the crêpe batter, trying not to create any bubbles. Heat a medium nonstick skillet or griddle over high heat for 3 to 4 minutes. You'll know when it's hot enough when a few droplets of water sizzle on the skillet. Working quickly, pour ¼ cup of batter onto the center of the skillet and spread into a large and thin circle with the back of the measuring cup or the back of a spoon (do it quickly—the batter cooks fast). Drizzle ¼ teaspoon of canola oil over the top of the crêpe. Cook the underside of the crêpe until browned, 1 to 1½ minutes. Flip and cook the other side until it's dry, about 30 seconds. Serve with a generous scoop of chutney and eat hot.

THE SMELL OF CHEELAS hot off the griddle is my favorite wake-up call. When I go home to visit my family in India, my mother makes them for me for breakfast. My father, Charlie, and I eat them as fast as possible, making sure that we each scoop up as much chutney in the cheelas as possible. Shallots lend a superb mild onion-garlic flavor to the chutney, but you can also substitute one medium red onion.

my french toast

SERVES 6 TO 8

12 large eggs
1/2 cup heavy cream
1/4 cup sugar
1 teaspoon vanilla bean paste, or
   1 1/2 teaspoons vanilla extract
1/2 teaspoon ground cardamom

Pinch of salt
1 stick unsalted butter, melted
1 loaf of day-old brioche or challah bread
   sliced 3/4 inch thick (about 8 to 10 slices)
3/4 cup demerara sugar

Preheat the oven to 200°F. Whisk the eggs, cream, sugar, vanilla bean paste, cardamom, and salt together in a large bowl.

Pool a little melted butter onto a serving platter or plates (the melted butter prevents the caramelized sugar from sticking to the plates) and set aside. Heat a griddle or large nonstick skillet over medium-high heat. Submerge 1 slice of bread in the egg mixture, turning the bread over to coat, and letting it get as soft as a wet sponge. Drizzle a little melted butter on the griddle, turn the heat down to medium, and place the soaked bread on the griddle. Sprinkle 2 teaspoons of sugar in an even layer over the bread. Once the bottom side is browned, flip and sprinkle the top with 2 teaspoons of sugar. When the bottom is browned, flip again, and wait until the sugar is browned before transferring to the platter or individual plate. If serving on a platter, keep the French toast warm in the oven while you repeat with the remaining bread slices.

THIS IS ONE of several Western dishes that my mother made for us kids in India. Instead of drowning our French toast in syrup, she would sprinkle coarse demerara sugar on the bread, so as it cooked on the grill, the sugar caramelized and pooled, creating a sticky, sweet, and crunchy built-in coating that we found addictive. I use vanilla paste in this recipe as I feel it provides a gentler, richer vanilla flavor than vanilla extract. If you don't have demerara sugar, replace it with citrus sugar: Pulse some sugar cubes with lemon or orange zest in your food processor and sprinkle over the French toast as it is cooking.

desserts

My sweet tooth is legendary among my friends and acquaintances. I may claim not to be hungry, but offer me dessert and suddenly I develop a ravenous appetite. It should be no surprise, then, that in my home, desserts are never neglected. If you visit us during one of the rare weeks when Charlie and I make a gallant effort to watch our diet and eat fewer sweets, you leave without a grudge, knowing that after a few days we'll be back in the kitchen, baking cakes and pies and making fresh-churned ice cream.

I blame my mother for my insatiable craving for dessert. Mom is a talented baker, and during our three years in Nagpur, even while balancing a tight budget and entertaining scores of visitors, she somehow always found the time and money to make desserts that comforted, nourished, and lavished us kids with affection and love. Sometimes they were just simple pound cakes while other times she fried the best donuts you could ever imagine.

Mom learned to bake from her teacher Mrs. Singh, one of the most famous Indian cookbook writers. While Mrs. Singh resided in England, she developed an affinity for Western sweets. In fact, as a result of two centuries of colonization and occupation, much of India, especially the elite social clubs, often serve Western savories and desserts. This love of cakes, cookies, tarts, and cobblers carries through to my home and my restaurant in New York City, where the pastry chef, my dear friend Surbhi Sahni, makes the most indulgent yet iconic desserts from India, like summer berry pudding, mango cheesecake, kulfi, and ice cream.

Nani's Pineapple Cake is a recipe that I learned from my nani, my grandmother, who certainly must have picked it up from a weathered *Ladies' Home Journal* or even a product label. It is so simple and easy that she would whip it together after dinner so it could be enjoyed while still warm. The Semolina Pudding is as Indian as apple pie is American. Considered a food of the gods, even though it never tastes quite as special as it does when eaten in a Sikh Gurdwara temple where it is offered in small tastes to devotees, when we make it at home, it is happily devoured.

If you want to spoil a loved one, do as Mom did and make donuts—you will see the recipient's eyes roll in delight! Even thirty years later, thinking about Mom's freshly fried donuts makes my mouth water.

With milk, heavy cream, eggs, cream cheese, vanilla beans, flour, and sugar in your cold and dry pantries, you will never find yourself at a loss for dessert. I hope that this chapter brings sweet endings to your table that serve as beginnings of new conversations and lifelong friendships.

semolina pudding (sooji ka halwa)

SERVES 6 TO 8

16 green cardamom pods, or ¾ teaspoon
  ground cardamom
4 cups water
¾ cup sugar

1 cup ghee or clarified butter
1 cup semolina flour
½ cup slivered almonds
½ cup golden raisins

Take 10 of the cardamom pods and separate the shells from the seeds; reserve 6 shells and set aside. Use a mortar and pestle or spice grinder to grind the cardamom seeds until they are powdery and fine and set it aside.

Pour the water into a medium saucepan. Add the sugar and the reserved 6 cardamom shells (if using whole cardamom pods) and bring to a boil. Reduce heat to low. Heat the ghee and the remaining 6 whole cardamom pods in a large pot or wok over medium-high heat for 1 minute. Reduce the heat to medium, add the semolina, and stir constantly for 4 minutes. Add the almonds and raisins and stir until the almonds are golden, 1½ to 2 minutes.

Skim the cardamom shells from the simmering water and discard. Stir the flavored water into the pot with the semolina and then add ½ of the ground cardamom. Cook until the pudding is very thick and you can see the individual grains of semolina, 4 to 5 minutes. Sprinkle the remaining cardamom over the top and serve the halwa in bowls.

NANI, MY MATERNAL GRANDMOTHER, used to make the best sooji ka halwa (Semolina Pudding). Halwa, along with potato-and-pea samosas, is a staple of monsoon season—as soon as one unleashed its wrath on New Delhi, one of these dishes would be made to lure my brother, sister, and me indoors. Mom always put me to work hand-grinding the cardamom. She said I was an expert grinder, making the powder finer than anyone else, but I think her real goal was to get me out of her way so she could make the halwa. I was her constant shadow, especially in the kitchen.

Most Indians consider the halwa that is served at Sikh temples the gold standard. Visitors eat buttery-rich halwa, a food of the gods, from the palms of their hand. Something about its warm, soft texture and the cold marble beneath your bare feet is transcendent.

nani's pineapple cake

SERVES 8

¾ cup plus ⅔ cup sugar
9 canned pineapple rings
4½ teaspoons orange marmalade
1⅓ cups all-purpose flour
1½ teaspoons baking powder
¾ teaspoon salt

1 stick plus 6 tablespoons unsalted butter,
 at room temperature
Zest of 2 lemons
4 large eggs
Vanilla ice cream, for serving

Preheat the oven to 350°F. Place ¾ cup of the sugar in a small saucepan over medium-high heat. Cover and cook the sugar until it begins to melt around the edges of the pan, 2 to 4 minutes. Remove the cover and swirl to redistribute the heat. Cover and continue to cook, swirling every 30 seconds, until the caramel is a deep reddish brown, 3 to 6 minutes longer. Pour the caramel into an 8 x 8-inch baking dish and let cool for a few minutes. Arrange the pineapple rings on top of the caramel in 3 rows (the pineapple will slightly overlap). Add ½ teaspoon of orange marmalade to the center of each pineapple ring and set the baking dish aside.

Sift the flour, baking powder, and salt together and set aside. With an electric mixer beat together the softened butter, remaining ⅔ cup of sugar, and lemon zest until creamy. Beat in the eggs one at a time, scraping the bowl between additions, until the mixture is thick and pale. Use a rubber spatula to gently mix in the flour until no dry patches remain.

Spread the batter over the pineapple rings and bake the cake for 35 to 40 minutes, or until the center of the cake springs back to light pressure. Immediately run a paring knife around the perimeter of the baking dish and invert the cake onto a platter. Serve warm or cold with vanilla ice cream.

NANI, MY MATERNAL GRANDMOTHER, used to whip this cake up after dinner and bake it while we all savored the very last morsels of the meal she prepared. She taught me to cover the saucepan while the sugar caramelizes, which traps condensation in the pan, preventing the sugar from crystallizing and making this method virtually foolproof. If you have never made caramel before, place a wide bowl filled with ice water next to your stovetop. Shock the bottom of the pan in the ice water to immediately stop the sugar from cooking. To clean the saucepan easily, fill it with water and bring the water to a boil. All of the hard sugar in the pan will dissolve effortlessly.

pistachio-and-cardamom pound cake with lemon icing

MAKES 1 LOAF

FOR THE CAKE

1 cup raw, shelled pistachios
1 stick plus 5 tablespoons unsalted butter,
    at room temperature
1 cup all-purpose flour
¾ teaspoon baking powder
1 teaspoon ground cardamom (preferably
    freshly ground)
¼ teaspoon salt
3 large eggs
¼ teaspoon vanilla extract
1 cup sugar
½ cup whole milk

FOR THE ICING

1 cup confectioners' sugar
1 teaspoon ground cardamom (preferably
    freshly ground)
1 tablespoon plus 1½ teaspoons fresh
    lemon juice
1 teaspoon heavy cream or milk

Preheat the oven to 425°F. To prepare the cake, place the pistachios on a rimmed baking sheet and toast until fragrant and browned, about 5 minutes. Cool and then pulse in a food processor until they become very fine (be careful not to overprocess; otherwise you'll have pistachio butter) and set aside. Reduce your oven temperature to 350°F.

Grease an 8½ x 4½-inch loaf pan with ½ tablespoon of butter. Place a long strip of parchment paper in the pan bottom. Grease the top of the parchment with ½ tablespoon of butter and set aside.

Whisk the flour, baking powder, cardamom, and salt together in a medium bowl and set aside. Crack the eggs into a liquid measuring cup, whisk in the vanilla, and set aside.

Using an electric mixer, cream the remaining stick and a half of butter and sugar until they are light and airy. Drizzle in the eggs, a little at a time, beating between additions to incorporate and scraping the bowl as necessary. Alternate adding the flour and the milk, starting and ending with the flour and mixing until the batter is just nearly combined between additions, scraping the bowl as necessary. Fold the pistachios into the batter by hand, then transfer the batter to the prepared loaf pan. Bake the cake until a cake tester inserted into the cake's center comes out clean, 45 to 55 minutes. Let the cake cool for 10 minutes, then invert the cake onto a cooling rack and turn it so its top faces up. Let the cake cool completely.

While the cake cools, make the icing: Sift the confectioners' sugar and cardamom into a medium bowl. Whisk in the lemon juice and cream or milk. Spread the icing over the cake, letting it drip over the sides. Once the icing has set, slice and serve.

THIS RECIPE COMES from Elie Nasr, whom I met through eGullet, a food Web site and chat group. Elie sent me his Lebanese mother's recipe for pistachio pound cake thinking I would enjoy it. He was right—I loved it from the first time that I baked it. It's incredibly tender and fine. I find that freshly ground cardamom enhances the flavor of the pistachios, contributing an ethereal citrus essence. The lemon icing is a nice finishing touch, but the cake is just as delicious plain. Heavy cream makes the icing opaque and less gritty, but if you don't have any handy, add an extra teaspoon of lemon juice.

chocolate hazelnut torte

MAKES ONE 8-INCH CAKE

FOR THE CAKE

1½ cups raw hazelnuts (or unsalted
    skinned hazelnuts)
9 tablespoons (1 stick plus 1 tablespoon)
    unsalted butter, at room temperature
8 ounces bittersweet chocolate (preferably
    between 80% and 85% cacao), finely
    chopped
¼ cup unbleached all-purpose flour
½ teaspoon ground ginger
¼ teaspoon ground cloves
¼ teaspoon cayenne pepper
¼ teaspoon salt
¾ cup sugar
3 large eggs, separated

FOR THE GLAZE

4 ounces bittersweet chocolate (preferably
    between 80% and 85% cacao), finely
    chopped
½ cup (1 stick) unsalted butter
1 tablespoon honey
¼ teaspoon cayenne pepper

Preheat the oven to 350°F. To make the cake, place the hazelnuts on a rimmed baking sheet and roast them until the skins are deep brown and the nuts smell toasted, 10 to 15 minutes. Cool, wrap the nuts in a kitchen towel, and rub them together to remove their skins. (If using skinned hazelnuts, then toast them for just 5 to 10 minutes, or until they smell nutty and set aside to cool completely.)

Grease an 8-inch cake pan with 1 tablespoon of butter and set aside.

Bring 2 inches of water to a boil in a medium saucepan and then reduce the heat to low. Place the chocolate in a large bowl and set over the hot water in the saucepan (the bottom of the bowl shouldn't touch the water). Stir occasionally until the chocolate is completely melted. Set aside to cool slightly.

Pulse 1 cup of the cooled hazelnuts in a food processor until they become very fine (be careful not to overprocess; otherwise you'll have hazelnut butter) and set aside. Sift the flour with the spices and salt and set aside. Chop the remaining hazelnuts coarsely and set aside.

Using an electric mixer, beat the remaining stick of butter with ½ cup of the sugar until the mixture is fluffy and pale, scraping the bowl as necessary. Beat in the egg yolks, one at a time, and then beat in the chocolate and the ground hazelnuts, scraping down the bowl as necessary.

In another bowl, beat the egg whites until they hold soft peaks. Add the remaining ¼ cup of sugar and beat until the egg whites regain their soft peaks. Using a rubber spatula, fold half of the whites into the chocolate mixture. Fold in the sifted flour mixture, and then the remaining egg whites, folding very gently until only a couple white streaks remain. Pour the batter into the prepared cake pan and bake until a cake tester comes out clean and the cake yields to light pressure, 30 to 40 minutes. Cool the cake in the pan on a wire rack for 15 minutes, run a paring knife around the pan edges, and invert the cake onto the wire rack to cool completely.

While the cake cools, make the glaze: Bring 2 inches of water to a simmer in a medium saucepan and reduce the heat to low. Place the chocolate, butter, honey, and cayenne pepper in a large bowl and set over the hot water in the saucepan (the bottom of the bowl shouldn't touch the water). Stir occasionally until all of the ingredients are melted and combined. Remove the bowl from on top of the saucepan and cool the mixture slightly so the glaze isn't too thin. Pour the glaze over the cooled cake, allowing it to run over the cake's sides. Sprinkle the top of the cake with the chopped hazelnuts and let the glaze set up for 1 hour before slicing and serving.

WHEN I LIVED in Greenwich Village, I had an Italian neighbor, Rick Turturro, who grew up on Long Island. It was no secret that Rick was not fond of Indian cuisine. One day, I invited him over for dinner, luring him by saying that I was making American food. The food came with an Indian accent, and Rick instantly fell in love with it. This cake was his contribution to the evening's meal—and I, in turn, fell in love with it, as it reminded me of the cake Neena Auntie used to make when I was a kid. I've added some spices that work nicely with chocolate. Use the best chocolate that is available to you— the better the chocolate, the better the cake. I like Scharffen Berger, El Ray, or Valrhona brands.

lemon raspberry cream cake

SERVES 8 TO 12

FOR THE RASPBERRY CURD
12 ice cubes
2 pints raspberries
3 large eggs plus 4 egg yolks
Zest and juice of 1 lemon
Pinch of salt
½ cup (1 stick) unsalted butter, cut into
    small pieces
½ cup sugar

1¼ cups all-purpose flour
½ teaspoon baking powder
¼ teaspoon baking soda
¼ teaspoon table salt
2 large eggs
½ cup sour cream
Juice of 1 lemon
1 cup plus 2 tablespoons sugar
1½ quarts (6 pints) raspberries

FOR THE CAKE
½ cup (1 stick) plus 1 tablespoon unsalted
    butter, at room temperature

FOR THE WHIPPED CREAM
1½ cups heavy cream
3 tablespoons sugar

To make the curd, place the ice cubes in a large bowl, cover with 6 cups of cold water, and set aside. Place the raspberries in a blender or food processor and puree. Transfer the raspberry puree to a medium bowl and whisk in the eggs and egg yolks, lemon zest and juice, and salt.

Melt the butter and sugar together using a double boiler or by placing the butter and sugar in a medium bowl and setting the bowl over a saucepan filled with 2 inches of simmering water (the bowl's bottom shouldn't touch the water). Stir occasionally until melted.

Slowly whisk in the raspberry mixture and cook while slowly stirring constantly until the raspberry mixture leaves a trail on the back of a spoon, 8 to 10 minutes. Place the bowl in your ice water bath (making sure no water gets into the raspberry curd), cover flush with plastic wrap, and transfer to the refrigerator to cool completely.

While the curd cools, make the cake: Heat your oven to 350°F. Grease a 9 x 11-inch baking dish with 1 tablespoon of butter and set aside. Sift the flour, baking powder, baking soda, and salt into a large bowl and then resift it over a sheet of parchment paper and then sift one more time back over the bowl.

Whisk the eggs, sour cream, and lemon juice together in a small bowl and set aside. Using an electric mixer, beat the remaining 1 stick of butter and 1 cup of sugar together until it is completely incorporated, about 2 minutes. Scrape down the sides of the bowl and reduce the mixer speed to low. Add a third of the flour, mixing until some dry patches remain. Add half of the sour cream mixture, mixing until just barely combined. Follow with half of the remaining flour mixture and once it is barely combined, add the remaining sour cream mixture. Add the remaining flour mixture, mixing by hand until it is just combined.

Transfer the batter to the prepared baking dish and spread as evenly as possible. Sprinkle with 2 tablespoons of sugar and bake until the cake bounces back under light pressure and a cake tester comes out with a crumb or two still attached, 20 to 25 minutes, turning midway through. Remove the cake from the oven and set aside to cool completely.

While the cake cools, make the whipped cream. Whip the heavy cream with 3 tablespoons of sugar until the cream can make soft peaks, 2 to 3 minutes.

Place 2 pints of raspberries in a small bowl and mash lightly with a fork. Spread evenly over the cake and cover with the raspberry curd, spreading it evenly over the raspberries. Spread an even layer of the whipped cream over the raspberry curd and decorate with the remaining 4 pints of raspberries. Refrigerate the cake for at least 8 hours or overnight before serving.

THIS IS MY TAKE on a cake that pastry chef extraordinaire Surbhi Sahni makes. Surbhi's desserts bring together flavors of the East and West in perfect harmony. The key to the light and airy cake base is sifting the flour at least three times (Surbhi and my mom both sometimes sift up to five times!), and for the tenderest cake possible, mix in the flour and liquid gently and until just barely incorporated. This is the kind of cake that is better the next day, so be sure to save the leftovers.

mixed-fruit cobbler

SERVES 8

FOR THE FRUIT

6 cups fruit (like apples, apricots,
   nectarines, peaches, pears, plums,
   rhubarb, or sour cherries), cut into thin
   wedges, slices, or halved (cherries)
3 cups berries (like blackberries,
   blueberries, boysenberries, raspberries,
   or strawberries)
1 cup sugar
1 teaspoon cornstarch
Zest of 1 lemon plus juice of 1/2 lemon
1/2 teaspoon ground ginger
1/4 teaspoon ground peppercorns
1/8 teaspoon cayenne pepper
Pinch of freshly grated nutmeg
Pinch of salt

FOR THE TOPPING

1 large egg
3 tablespoons whole milk or heavy cream
1 cup all-purpose flour
4 tablespoons sugar
1 1/2 teaspoons baking powder
1/2 teaspoon salt
6 tablespoons (3/4 stick) frozen butter, cut
   into small pieces
Heavy cream, whipped cream, or vanilla
   ice cream, for serving

Preheat the oven to 375°F. To prepare the fruit, combine the fruit and berries in a large bowl and toss together with the sugar, cornstarch, lemon zest, spices, and salt. Transfer the fruit to a large pot and cook over medium-high heat until the fruit breaks down into a jamlike consistency, about 5 minutes, stirring once or twice. Spread the fruit in a 9 x 11-inch baking dish and set aside.

To make the topping, whisk together the egg and milk and set aside. Place the flour, 2 table-spoons of the sugar, baking powder, and salt in a food processor and pulse to combine. Add the butter and pulse until the butter is worked in, and there are no bits larger than a small pea. Add the liquid to the dry ingredients while pulsing until all of the liquid is added and just a couple of dry patches remain. Transfer the dough to a large bowl and work by hand once or twice just to combine.

Break the dough into 12 small chunks, and arrange them over the fruit. Sprinkle the biscuits with the remaining 2 tablespoons sugar. Bake the cobbler until the biscuits are golden brown, 25 to 30 minutes. Remove from the oven and let cool for at least 30 minutes. Serve with heavy cream or ice cream.

EVER SINCE CHARLIE and I met, cobblers have been a mainstay in our kitchen. We got our recipe from Charlie's grandmother Burd, who made cobblers for Charlie when he was a young boy. Foolproof and incredibly easy, it will become a recipe you turn to, time and time again. Cooking the fruit on the stovetop before baking develops its flavor and thickness. It's an extra step, but one well worth taking. I like my cobbler with a scoop of vanilla ice cream, and Charlie likes his how Grandma made it for him—with milk or cream poured over the top.

mom's donuts

MAKES ABOUT 20 DONUTS

Canola oil, for deep frying
2 cups all-purpose flour plus extra, for
    dusting work surface
1½ teaspoons baking powder
½ teaspoon salt
½ teaspoon ground ginger
½ teaspoon freshly grated nutmeg

¼ teaspoon cinnamon
1 large egg
½ cup plain whole milk yogurt
2½ cups sugar
Zest of 1 lemon
½ teaspoon baking soda

Heat enough canola oil to fill a medium saucepan by 3 inches to 350°F.

Sift the flour, baking powder, salt, ginger, nutmeg, and cinnamon into a large bowl. In a medium bowl, whisk together the egg, yogurt, ½ cup of the sugar, and the lemon zest. Add the baking soda and whisk to combine (the mixture should get bubbly). Add the yogurt mixture to the dry ingredients and stir to combine. The dough will be very wet and tacky. Place the remaining 2 cups of sugar on a large plate or in a baking dish and set aside.

Sprinkle a generous amount of flour onto your work surface. Transfer the dough ball to your work surface and sprinkle flour over it. Pat it with your hands into a thin disc, ¼ to ⅓ inch thick. Use a 2- to 3-inch round cookie cutter (or upturned coffee mug) to cut circles out of the dough. Use a 1-inch cookie cutter (or bottle cap) to cut small circles from the center of each larger dough circle. Place the donut shapes onto a plate and repat the dough scraps into a large circle, cutting out more donuts (you should get about 15 to 20 donuts, depending on the size of the cookie cutter you use).

Fry 4 to 6 donuts at a time, turning them often and basting them with the hot oil, 2 to 2½ minutes, or until they're evenly browned all over. Repeat with the remaining donuts. Place the hot donuts in the reserved sugar while still hot and turn to coat. Eat hot, or within a couple of hours of frying.

DONUTS BRING BACK some of my fondest childhood memories, with Mom throwing this dough together in minutes, and we kids gobbling up the sugar-tossed donuts as quickly as she made them. Mom made donuts while we lived in Nagpur; since we had no cookie cutters, we'd use a jam jar lid and a ketchup bottle cap to stamp out the donut and its inner ring. When Karun, my six-year-old nephew, visits Mom in India, she reignites her donut prowess and makes these. Leavened by baking powder and a baking soda-yogurt emulsion, they're light and crispy and absolutely phenomenal. If you're using a high-protein flour like King Arthur or Hecker's, then add 2 tablespoons of yogurt and ⅛ teaspoon of baking soda to the mix.

fig flan

SERVES 8 TO 10

4 dried figs (about 3 ounces), finely
   chopped
1½ cups half-and-half
¼ cup dark rum
1 (14-ounce) can sweetened condensed
   milk

4 large eggs
8 ounces cream cheese
2 tablespoons fig jam
1 cup sugar
¼ cup water
A 1-inch piece cinnamon stick

Set an oven rack to the lowest position and preheat your oven to 350°F. Place the figs, half-and-half, and rum in a medium saucepan and bring to a boil. Turn off the heat, cover the pan, and steep the figs for 10 minutes.

Place the condensed milk, eggs, cream cheese, and fig jam in a blender and blend until smooth, about 2 minutes. Add the half-and-half, figs, and rum, and blend until they are completely incorporated.

Bring the sugar, water, and cinnamon stick to a simmer in a medium, heavy-bottomed saucepan and remove the pan from the heat. Stir until the sugar is dissolved and the syrup is clear. Return the saucepan to the heat and bring the liquid to a boil, swirling the pan every now and then, until the syrup caramelizes to a deep brown, 4 to 5 more minutes. Immediately pour the caramel into a 2½-quart metal charlotte mold or a 9 x 5-inch loaf pan. Carefully remove the cinnamon stick with a spoon or tongs. Tip the mold or pan to coat the bottom and sides with the caramel. Let it cool for a few minutes and then pour the custard mixture into it.

Line an 8-inch square baking pan (or a larger rectangular baking pan, if using a loaf pan) with a doubled kitchen towel. Put the mold in the baking pan on top of the towel and then place the pan into the oven. Use a cup to add hot water to the baking pan, adding enough water to reach the middle of the mold or loaf pan. Bake the flan until the custard is set but still jiggles when shaken and a skewer stuck into the flan about 1 inch from the pan edge comes out clean, about 1 hour and 25 minutes.

Carefully lift the mold out of the pan. Turn off the oven and let the water in the baking dish cool a little before removing it. Refrigerate the flan until it is completely chilled.

To serve, set the mold over direct heat until the bottom gets hot, about 1 minute. (This is to melt the bottom layer of caramel so that the flan will slip out of the mold.) Run a knife around the edge of the flan to loosen it from the mold. Place a serving platter over the mold and then invert the mold onto the platter. Lift off the mold. Cut the flan into wedges or slices and serve.

THIS RECIPE CAME about after Charlie discovered a wonderfully delicious bottle of fig jam in our pantry. It was a bitter winter morning and with no fruit in the house and little else around to create something special, we turned to the fig jam to sate our sweet tooth. Charlie thought of my flan base and to that we added the jam and some Kashmiri dried figs we had been guarding with the utmost care since our visit to the region during the winter of 2005. The flan turned out to be shockingly good and we now serve it regularly, thinking fondly of the snow-capped Himalayas and fig trees whenever we do. If you can't find fig jam, instead double the amount of dried figs in the recipe.

magic bars

MAKES 16 BARS

1½ cups (3 sticks) unsalted butter, melted, plus 1 tablespoon, for greasing the baking dish
1 (14.4-ounce) box graham crackers
1 cup slivered almonds, toasted
8 ounces chocolate (milk, semisweet, or bittersweet), finely chopped
6 ounces white chocolate, finely chopped
1 cup shredded sweetened coconut

1½ cups Mixed Nut Brittle (page 251), or 1½ cups roughly chopped and toasted chopped nuts plus ½ cup roughly chopped chocolate-covered toffee (such as a Heath Bar)
½ cup roughly chopped toasted nuts (pistachios, slivered almonds, pecans, peanuts)
1 (14-ounce) can sweetened condensed milk

Preheat the oven to 350°F. Grease a 9 x 11-inch baking dish with butter and set aside.

Using a food processor, grind the graham crackers and almonds together to make fine crumbs. Place the crumbs in a medium bowl and mix in the melted butter. Transfer to the prepared baking dish, pat into an even, firm layer, and set aside.

Mix the chocolates with the coconut, Nut Brittle, chopped nuts, and condensed milk in a large bowl. Pour over the crust and bake until the chocolate is partially melted and the coconut is browned, about 20 minutes. Cool overnight before cutting into squares.

I LOVE TEASING my dear friend Matt Grady, coauthor Raquel's husband and a true urbanite, about his rural upbringing in New Hampshire. One of his sweetest childhood memories is of these bar cookies, which his mother, Billie, always brings when she visits New York. While we were neighbors in Brooklyn, Matt and Raquel happily shared Billie's magic bars with us. Charlie grew to be especially fond of them, and Billie now knows to bring a box especially for him. The key is to let the bars cool overnight (which takes the utmost willpower) so they bind together and cut easily into neat squares. Gooey, crunchy, brittle, and nutty, these bars really invoke sugar-induced euphoria. Though you can make them with store-bought chocolate-covered toffee, they are absolutely amazing made with the Mixed Nut Brittle. They can last for 1 week (or more) stored in a covered plastic container.

raquel's sticky toffee cake

SERVES 8

FOR THE PUDDING

4 tablespoons (½ stick) unsalted butter,
    melted, plus 1 tablespoon, for greasing
    the baking dish
1¼ cups all-purpose flour
½ teaspoon baking powder
½ teaspoon salt
1½ cups pitted dates
1 cup sugar

2 large eggs
1¼ cups warm water
1 teaspoon vanilla extract

FOR THE SAUCE

½ cup (1 stick) unsalted butter
1 cup packed dark brown sugar
¾ cup heavy cream
2 tablespoons brandy or rum (optional)

Preheat the oven to 350°F. To make the pudding, grease an 8 x 8-inch baking dish with butter and set aside. Whisk the flour, baking powder, and salt together in a medium bowl.

Combine the dates and sugar in a food processor with three 1-second pulses. Add the eggs, warm water, and vanilla and process until smooth. With the food processor running, add the melted butter through the feed tube and then transfer the batter to a large bowl.

Whisk the flour into the batter in three additions. Pour the batter into the prepared baking dish and bake until the center of the cake bounces back to light pressure, 25 to 30 minutes, rotating the cake midway through cooking.

While the cake cooks, make the sauce: Melt the butter in a medium saucepan over medium-high heat. Reduce the heat to medium and whisk in the brown sugar. Cook, stirring occasionally, until the sugar is completely dissolved, 4 to 5 minutes. Whisk in the cream and brandy (if using) and simmer until it is slightly thickened, about 3 minutes.

Remove the cake from the oven (leave the oven on) and prick it all over with a wooden skewer down to the bottom of the pan. Pour ½ of the sauce over the top of the cake and spread it evenly with a spatula. Bake for an additional 5 minutes. Remove from the oven, cool, and cut into squares. Serve with the remaining sauce on the side.

WHEN RAQUEL AND MATT were our neighbors in Brooklyn's historic Clinton Hill (a short-lived adventure that I will always remember fondly), I relied on Raquel to make her toffee "pudding" for get-togethers. Easy to make and delicious beyond compare, it's a dessert that you, too, will get hooked on quickly. In fact, I now ask her to double the recipe and make a giant batch so I am sure to have leftovers all to myself the next day. The dates should be very soft and sticky; if the ones you buy are dry and hard, you're better off making the cake with dried figs, apricots, or a combination of dried fruits.

chocolate ice cream

MAKES ABOUT 1¼ QUARTS

3 cups half-and-half, or 1½ cups whole
   milk plus 1½ cups heavy cream
7 ounces bittersweet chocolate (preferably
   80% to 85% cacao), finely chopped

5 egg yolks
1 cup sugar
⅛ teaspoon salt

Pour the half-and-half into a medium heavy-bottomed saucepan and bring to a simmer over medium-high heat. Remove the pan from the heat, add the chocolate, and whisk until it is completely melted and the mixture is smooth.

Bring 2 inches of water to a simmer in a medium saucepan and reduce the heat to medium-low. Whisk the egg yolks with the sugar and salt in a large bowl until thoroughly combined. Gradually whisk in the chocolate mixture, mixing until incorporated. Place the bowl on top of the saucepan (the bottom of the bowl should not touch the water) and stir constantly with a wooden spoon until you can draw a clear line through the custard on the back of the spoon, about 10 minutes. Cover the chocolate custard flush with plastic wrap and refrigerate the custard until it's cold.

Transfer the custard to an ice-cream maker and process it according to the manufacturer's instructions. Transfer the ice cream to a container, cover it, and freeze until the ice cream is firm, at least 4 hours or up to 3 days. Let the ice cream stand at room temperature for 5 to 10 minutes before scooping and serving.

THIS IS, HANDS-DOWN, the richest chocolate ice cream that you will ever make or taste. It will spoil you for a lifetime. The trick is to use the best chocolate you can find —my absolute favorite splurge is to use Debauve & Gallais chocolate. Take care not to scald or burn the chocolate as this can change the chocolate's flavor and texture. Ensure that the water under the double boiler is simmering gently and not touching the chocolate bowl's bottom and you should be fine. Add nuts, good-quality chocolate chips or chunks, chocolate shavings, or even some chilled chocolate sauce to the ice cream as it is churning for an even more decadent scoop.

vanilla ice cream

MAKES ABOUT 1¼ QUARTS

1 vanilla bean, or 1 teaspoon vanilla paste
   or vanilla extract
12 ice cubes

3 cups half-and-half, or 1½ cups whole
   milk plus 1½ cups heavy cream
6 egg yolks
¾ cup sugar

Cut a vanilla bean in half lengthwise. Using the tip of the knife, scrape the seeds into a small bowl and set aside. Place the ice cubes in a large bowl with 4 cups of water, place a medium metal bowl in the ice water bath, and set aside.

Pour the half-and-half into a medium heavy-bottomed saucepan and bring to a simmer. Turn off the heat and whisk in the reserved vanilla seeds and bean. Cover the saucepan and let the mixture stand for 30 minutes.

Meanwhile, whisk the egg yolks with the sugar in a large bowl until thoroughly combined. Remove the vanilla bean from the half-and-half. Pour the liquid through a sieve and into the eggs a little at a time, whisking constantly. (You can skip this step if you're using vanilla paste or extract.)

Return the egg mixture to the saucepan and place it over medium-high heat. Cook, stirring slowly and continuously with a wooden spoon or whisk until you can draw a clear line through the custard on the back of the spoon, about 5 minutes. Do not allow the custard to boil, as this could cause the eggs to curdle.

Pour the custard through a medium-mesh sieve and into the chilled metal bowl in the water bath. Whisk for 30 seconds to cool slightly. Cover the custard flush with plastic wrap and refrigerate it (you can leave it in the ice water bath if you like) until it's cold, about 1 hour. Transfer the custard to an ice-cream maker and freeze it according to the manufacturer's instructions. Transfer the ice cream to a container, cover, and freeze until the ice cream is firm, at least 4 hours or up to 3 days. Let the ice cream stand at room temperature for 5 to 10 minutes before scooping and serving.

VARIATION: Rum Raisin Ice Cream

Soak ½ cup of raisins in 3 tablespoons of rum for at least 1 hour, or preferably overnight. Once the ice cream is just about done churning, add the raisins and churn 1 minute more. Transfer it to a container, cover, and freeze. Since this ice cream contains alcohol, it will remain slightly soft.

CRÈME ANGLAISE, the base of this ice cream, is a lot easier to prepare and a lot less dramatic than most chefs would have you think. If you stand in front of your stove, and make sure you are whisking away, the custard rarely curdles. If it does, force it through a sieve (a step that I included in the recipe yet rarely ever do unless teaching a class) and your ice cream base is, once again, as right as rain.

With this base, you can make countless variations. Cook peaches, strawberries, or sour cherries with some sugar and a little lemon juice until softened, cool, and add 1 cup at the end of churning. Bits of Mixed Nut Brittle (page 251) add an excellent crunch, while Candied Orange Peel (page 248) contributes a sophisticated bittersweet flavor.

pavlova with spiced berries and cointreau cream

SERVES 8

FOR THE MERINGUE
4 large egg whites
1 cup superfine sugar
2 teaspoons balsamic vinegar
1 tablespoon cornstarch

FOR THE FRUIT
2 pints strawberries, hulled and sliced
2 pints raspberries
1 pint blueberries
1 pint blackberries
1 cup sugar

$\frac{1}{3}$ teaspoon ground peppercorns
$\frac{1}{8}$ teaspoon cayenne pepper
1 tangerine, zested and juiced, with zest reserved for cream

FOR THE CREAM
1 cup heavy cream
2 tablespoons confectioners' sugar
1 tablespoon Cointreau
Tangerine zest, reserved from fruit mixture

Preheat your oven to 275°F. Line a baking sheet with parchment paper and set it aside.

To make the meringue, use an electric mixer to beat the egg whites with the superfine sugar and vinegar until soft peaks form. Sift the cornstarch over the whites and gently fold the two together with a rubber spatula. Spoon the meringue mixture onto the prepared baking sheet making eight equal dollops, leaving 2 inches between each. Using a circular motion, flatten the dollops into 4-inch-thick discs with the back of a spoon. Bake the meringues for 2 hours and then turn the oven off and let the meringues sit in the oven for another hour. Transfer the baking sheet to a wire rack and cool the meringues to room temperature.

While the meringues bake, make the fruit mixture: Place the berries, sugar, ground peppercorns, cayenne pepper, and tangerine juice in a large bowl and toss to combine. Cover with plastic wrap and refrigerate for at least 1 hour and up to 4 hours.

To make the cream, beat the cream, sugar, Cointreau, and tangerine zest together until stiff peaks form. Place the meringues on a platter or on individual plates. Spread each with cream and top with all but 1 cup of the macerated berries. Place some of the remaining berries on each plate and serve.

PAVLOVAS ARE A LOVELY, light dessert that seem to be popular everywhere except the United States. This is a pity, since they are so simple to make. The crispness of the meringue against the intensity of the fruit and richness of the spiked cream is stunning. You can make one large pavlova instead of individual ones; note that you may need to bake the meringue little longer.

cardamom-scented rice cream with saffron drizzle (firni)

SERVES 6

5 cups cold water
¼ cup raw basmati rice
4 cups half-and-half
¾ cup sugar
6 whole green cardamom pods, seeds
  removed and ground in a spice grinder

or using a mortar and pestle (or
⅓ teaspoon ground cardamom)
½ teaspoon saffron threads
2 tablespoons heavy cream

Combine the water and rice in a large bowl and let the rice soak overnight. The next day, transfer ¼ cup of the rice water to a blender. Drain the remaining water from the rice and place the rice in the blender. Grind the rice as finely as possible, scraping down the sides of the blender jar as necessary.

Bring the half-and-half to a simmer in a large heavy-bottomed saucepan. Add 1 cup of the half-and-half to the blender and pulse to release some steam, then blend for 10 seconds to combine. Transfer the contents of the blender to the saucepan and bring to a simmer over medium heat. Reduce the heat to low and stir constantly until the rice cream is as thick as a thin pudding and a trail can be made through the cream on the back of a spoon, 16 to 18 minutes (if the mixture foams up in the saucepan, remove the saucepan from the heat for a few seconds, reduce the heat, and continue to cook). Remove the saucepan from the heat and stir in the sugar and cardamom. Divide between 6 small glasses or ramekins and cool to room temperature. Cover each glass or dish with plastic wrap pressed directly onto the surface and chill at least 4 hours or up to 1 day.

Place the saffron in a small skillet and toast over low heat until the saffron threads are fragrant and darker in color, about 3 minutes. Transfer to a small bowl or to a mortar to cool, and then grind with the back of a teaspoon or with a pestle until powder-fine. Add the heavy cream. Drizzle some saffron sauce over each serving and serve immediately or chill up to 4 hours.

CREAMY AND luscious, firni, a smooth rice pudding, is the Indian version of Mahalabiya, a Middle Eastern dessert. Made from rice soaked in water overnight, ground in a blender and then simmered with half-and-half until thick, it is often made in the Middle East from cornstarch or a cornstarch-and-rice flour combination and flavored with rose water or orange blossom water. Mine is infused with freshly ground cardamom and finished with a vibrant saffron sauce. Served in shot glasses with tiny spoons, it's an elegant ending to any meal. Save leftover saffron sauce to flavor mashed potatoes, scrambled eggs, risotto, or a vanilla ice cream base.

candied orange peel

MAKES ABOUT 1 CUP

2 large oranges
2¾ cups sugar
9 cups ¾ cup water

4 whole cloves
2 green cardamom pods, crushed

Use a channel knife (a V-shaped zester) or vegetable peeler to peel off thin strips of peel from the oranges (you should get about 40 strips from each orange). Take care to remove just the orange zest and none of the white pith, which is very bitter.

Bring 3 cups of water to a boil in a medium saucepan. Add the orange peels and simmer for 10 minutes. Drain the water and add another 3 cups of water. Bring to a boil, simmer for 10 minutes, and drain. Repeat with another 3 cups of water.

Place ¾ cup of sugar and ¾ cup of water in a small saucepan. Bring it to a boil, stirring occasionally to dissolve the sugar, and add the cloves and the cardamom pods, mashing the cardamom pods into the bottom of the pot so they release their flavor. Add the orange peels and boil 25 minutes.

Place 2 cups of sugar on a baking sheet. Use a slotted spoon to remove the peel from the saucepan and place it on top of the sugar. Roll the peels in the sugar, shaking the baking sheet to make sure that each peel is completely coated (if the sugar becomes too wet, add more sugar to the baking sheet). Store the peel in a glass jar for up to 2 weeks.

THIS IS A RECIPE that I learned from my dear and loyal friend Naushab. Always the one to arrive early for parties at our home, he is also always the last to leave. He has a way about him that speaks of his thoughtful upbringing, patience, generosity, and rich Pakistani heritage. Originally from Lahore (fabled to be the Paris of the East), he has every bit of the Lahore charm that my grandparents' generation spoke of. Naushab makes Candied Orange Peel as a gift during the holidays. It's also a lovely hostess gift. Chopped finely, it's a nice addition to chocolate and vanilla ice cream. This is really a gift that never stops giving—after boiling the orange peel, save the simple syrup and the sugar left over from sugaring the peels for sweetening lemonade, iced tea, fresh fruit, or cocktails.

mixed nut brittle

MAKES ABOUT 3½ CUPS

1 tablespoon unsalted butter, at room
   temperature, for greasing
3 cups raw chopped or whole nuts
   (slivered almonds, cashews, peanuts,
   pecans, pistachios, or walnuts)

4 cups sugar

Preheat the oven to 375°F. Grease a rimmed baking sheet with 1 tablespoon of butter and set aside. Place the nuts on a rimmed baking sheet and roast them until they're fragrant and lightly toasted, about 5 minutes. Transfer to a bowl and set aside to cool.

Place the sugar in a large, heavy-bottomed pot over medium heat. Stir the sugar every few minutes to break up any lumps until the sugar is dissolved. Cover the pot (the condensation prevents the sugar from crystallizing) and cook, stirring every 2 minutes, for 10 to 12 minutes, or until the sugar is between amber and brown. Remove the cover, increase the heat to medium-high, and add the nuts. Stir to incorporate completely and then carefully transfer the hot Nut Brittle to the greased baking sheet. Using a rubber spatula spread the brittle into a ½-inch-thick layer. Set aside to cool completely and then chop into chunks. Stored in a sealed container, Nut Brittle lasts for weeks.

THIS IS MY MOTHER'S nut brittle recipe. She would usually make it with peanuts as they were readily available and usually quite inexpensive in India. Our home was like Grand Central Station—at every meal, there was a battalion of young and hungry stomachs to feed. Nut Brittle was a fast and easy sweet to offer us kids, and it even provided a bit of nutrition from the nuts. In commercial establishments in India, it is common to add dried rose petals and even saffron to the brittle. If using saffron, toast it for a few seconds in a dry skillet and then grind it into a powder. Toss the toasted saffron powder (or rose petals) with the toasted nuts before you add them to the caramel.

resources

Here are a few of my favorite sources for food items and kitchenware. Thanks to all of them for their generous contributions to this book.

CHEESES

Consider Bardwell Farm
Fresh chèvre, aged goat's and cow's milk cheeses, goat's milk feta
www.considerbardwellfarm.com
802-645-9928

MEATS

Jamison Farm
Naturally raised lamb from Pennsylvania
www.jamisonfarm.com
800-237-5762

COOKWARE AND TABLEWARE

My home would be incomplete both functionally and from a design standpoint if not for the beautifully designed and carefully crafted cookware and tableware that I collect.

ALL-CLAD METALCRAFTERS
www.allclad.com
800-ALL-CLAD

EMILE HENRY
I admire the color and range of shapes and sizes of Emile Henry's ovenware-to-tableware collection. They are pretty and practical.
www.emilehenry.com
302-326-4800

LE CREUSET
www.lecreuset.com
877-CREUSET

LODGE CAST IRON
www.lodgemfg.com
423-837-7181

MAUVIEL
Copperware is my favorite type of cookware. It is a durable and attractive investment that will last you a lifetime.
www.mauviel.com
302-326-4803

KITCHEN TOOLS

OXO Good Grips
www.oxo.com
800-545-4411

VITA-MIX PROFESSIONAL SERIES BLENDERS
www.theprofessionalseries.com
877-848-2649

KITCHEN APPLIANCES

Viking Range Corporation
www.vikingrange.com
888-VIKING1

SPICES, AROMATICS, AND ALL THINGS EXOTIC

Poha, chickpea flour, curry leaves, dried red chiles, fenugreek leaves, chaat masala, sambhaar, rasam, and all kinds of whole spices, seeds, and ground spices can be ordered from these sources. Order curry leaves in bulk and freeze them; they will keep for months.

ETHNICGROCER.COM
www.ethnicgrocer.com

FOODS OF INDIA
This is the temple of spice in the United States. They deliver across the country. Better quality is hard to come by even in India; in fact their selection is so fresh that my mother has been known to shop for spices here and take them back to New Delhi.
121 Lexington Avenue (between 28th and 29th Streets)
New York, NY 10016
212-683-4419

BAKING CHOCOLATES

My favorite companies, in order:

SCHARFFEN BERGER
www.scharffenberger.com
510-981-4044

DEBAUVE & GALLAIS
www.debauveandgallais.com
212-734-8880

EL REY
www.chocolates-elrey.com
830-997-2200

VALRHONA
www.valrhona.com

acknowledgments

American Masala truly is the essence of my life. It brings to fruition what I have learned and loved in India and in America. None of this would have been possible had it not been for the friends and family scattered across numerous continents. Your heroic efforts to keep in touch and share your recipes with me will always be remembered. Please celebrate yourself and our common affection for food, culture, and the people who brought us together.

Without my agent and dear friend, Angela Miller, and her husband, Russell Glover, this book might never have been anything but a dream. Angela juggles numerous responsibilities tirelessly; I strive to emulate how she manages her time while nourishing so many lives. I can never thank her and Russell enough for all they have shared. My editor, Pam Krauss, stood by me, championed my cuisine and my passion when even I did not know what tangible recipes lay hidden in my heart and history. She has great vision and endless literary and kitchen wisdom. Marysarah Quinn and Maggie Hinders; Lauren Shakely, publisher of Clarkson Potter; and Jenny Frost, president of Crown Publishing Group, have been steadfast in their support. Ben Fink contributed his brilliant photography and friendship. Andria Chin and Laura Lehrman of Lehrman+ Chin PR indefatigably dedicate themselves to the cause of Indian food and back every dream and menu change that I present to them.

At the home front, Charlie Burd, my partner in life and crime, has a way of turning my kaleidoscopic visions into ordered realty. He makes the undoable achievable and creates order from my chaos. Though our partnership may never find a worthy name owing to politics, it is as true and universal as any spousal relationship could ever be. Kali and Simba, our cats, keep me inspired, if only because my allergies to them keep me out of bed and on the computer. Sebastian and Aasha, our mighty mutts, are gourmands beyond most humans.

It was a treat when my sister, Seema; brother-in-law, Ajit; and nephew, Karun, moved to New York City. Karun is the joy that I look forward to after physically tiring travels. His smile, spirit, and own desire to be a chef keep me inspired. Beyond their appetites and unconditional encouragement, Seema and Ajit have provided every cushion of comfort and support that one could wish for. My brother, Samir, is a friend, a sibling, and a pillar of strength and support, rising to any challenge. He helps me stick to my course and shares in our family's commitment to culture and history. Old-fashioned values are alive and well in the home my brother and his wife, Radha, share with my parents in India. My parents should be proud of what they instilled in us kids, for no matter how much bickering we indulge in, at the end of the day, we are delighted to have one anothers' company.

Mom and Dad are an unending beacon of light for me and countless others. Through their own caring example they have made a compelling and concrete example of what it is to love and what it truly means to nourish. I only wish more people had such exemplary others in their lives. I will always be indebted to Panditji, who filled my early years with tasty food and beautiful historical anecdotes of our family history and that of India. His blessings are endless and impossible ever to share fully; his is a legacy that shall outlive us both. Chotu, Neera, Khaggi, Ram, and Maya have filled our home in Delhi with their love and sweat, and for that I shall always be grateful. The one person who combines the stature of all of my grandparents is my nana (maternal grandfather), Chaman Lal Bhardwaj. He is the rarest gem of a man, one who could put the most able statesman to shame with his knowledge, sophistication, understanding of life, religion, and culture and his undying, epic love of my enchanting grandmother. Thanks also to my elders, aunties, uncles, and family members near and far, who keep love and friendship alive and meaningful.

Kumkum Bhasin and Hari give me comfort and strength, believing in me always. Marina Ahmad Alam and Shantanu have kept my love of music and all things secular alive and kicking. When in need for new faith in life and humanity, all I need to do is to hear Marina sing, and I believe again. The very best of hosts, Renee and Carl Behnke; my first and still much loved American friend, Mary Ann Joulwan; forever dependable and dear, Naushab Ahmed; the incomparably generous, always indulgent, and forever reliable friends Kaka and Nalin; Gael Greene and Steven Richter; Michael and Arianne Batterberry; Bim and Monsoon Bissell; Rohit Bal; Elaine Hayes and Beth Burd; Ann and Richard Wilder; Maricel and Alex; Sherry Govender; Peter Daems; Patricia Quintana; Zarela Martinez; Grace Young; Najmieh Batmanglij; Andrew Zimmern; Zoe Francois; Daisy Martinez; Linda O'Keefe; Gil Daniel; Joe Dolce; Abhimanyu Katyal; Salma Abdelnour; Nancy Novogrod; Denise Gee and Bobby Peacock; Nora Carey; John Ochse; Susan Jardina; Gretchen Holt; Greg Drescher and Mai Pham; Anisha Mehra; Sandeep Solomon and Vanessa Baker; Aunty Raj, Sheeli, Rakesh, Rohan, and Paayal Aggarwal; Martha Jo Katz; Holly Briwa; Shashi Tharoor; Ramu Damodaran; Anita Trehan; Arun Sinha; Bala Krishna Pillai; Ralf Beuschlein; Ann and Damian Didden; Scott Hunt; Jim Poris; Beverly Stephen; Mohit, Shivani, and Aashika Jain; Sandeep and Abu; Vibhuti Patel; Martha Holmberg; Maria Hunt; Kimberley Davis; David Karp; Diane Chamberlain; Rohit Turkhud; Yvan Lemoine; Sal Rizzo and Gary Portuesi; Bernice Burd and Morris Alderman; David Guas and Simone Rathle; Manjula and Sandeep Mathur; Tina DeGraff; Salim Patel; Colin Cowie; Jason, Michael, and Meredith Brody; Rachna Iyer; Karen Page and Andrew Dornenburg; Shelley and Donald Rubin; Holly Johnsen;

Gary Danko; Joanne Weir; Barbara Buzzell; Carlyn Steiner; Joanne Ellis; Jan Whitsitt; Rosie and Neville; Wendell the Man and Amy; Lauren and Roger; Abhijit Saha; Anne Rawlings; Richard Arakelian; Lisa Larsen Hill; Donna and Tom; Mohamed Kourouma; Francisco Almada; Vicky Haupt; Namrata and Vivek; Sonia and Avinash Bal; Lily Kumari Gupta; Kate and Paul (for opening home, heart, country, and more); Chuck Edwards; Arlene and Alain; Martha Foose; Mark Bittman; Stephanie Lyness; Judy Short; Ashish and Candace; Charles, Leone, and Nathan Burd; Bret Bannon and Jon Templeton; Arlene Spiegel; Sushil and Elizabeth Patel; Guneet and Bubbly Bajwa; Art and Jesus; Chandra Ram, and countless dear friends and acquaintances.

In the professional realm I owe much to my co-chef and dear friend, Hemant Mathur. Many of my travels around the world to teach others about Indian cooking would not have been possible had it not been for him. Hemant translates my ideas into tangible dishes and has been a loyal partner for many years. His wife, the talented pastry chef Surbhi Sahni, has given me new friendship and their daughter, Soumyaa, sweeter moments still. Our restaurant staff work so hard each day delivering the very best in food and hospitality to everyone who walks through our door. For that commitment I thank each of them.

These recipes would never have been documented had it not been for the contributions of my coauthor Raquel's family. My dear friend and Raquel's husband, Matt Grady, is brilliant in too many ways to list. Julian, Matt and Raquel's son, born while we wrote this book, kept us in synch with what really matters. I am forever thankful to Raquel's parents, Josef Pelzel and Lauren Sayre, and her in-laws, Billie and Jerry Dionne, and Mike and Caren Grady for supporting this book in countless ways.

Lastly, *American Masala* is everything I want it to be because of the efforts of Raquel Pelzel. She ensured that no details were ever compromised and worked hard at my side to document every subtlety and relate each of my many anecdotes. Raquel, thanks for your partnership. Words could never share my full appreciation for your efforts   —SUVIR SARAN

Thanks to the powers that be for the blackout of 2003. Had the lights not gone out, I may not have met Suvir and Charlie, two of the best friends anyone could hope for, or the ever-wise Angela Miller and Pam Krauss. For his contagious calm, I am indebted to my husband, Matt, and for his remarkable flexibility during his first year on earth, my son, Julian.

Suvir, our relationship has been one of kismet from the start. This book is not only a reflection of your spirit and talent but of your loyalty and love for those around you. I am constantly in awe of your boundless ambition and generosity. Thank you for adding a pinch of masala (and your corn bread) to my life.   —RAQUEL PELZEL

index